FLY CASTING
scandinavian style

FLY CASTING
scandinavian style

Henrik Mortensen

STACKPOLE
BOOKS

Copyright 2010 Henrik Mortensen
Original edition copyright 2006 © Henrik Mortensen
Published by
STACKPOLE BOOKS
5067 Ritter Road
Mechanicsburg, PA 17055
www.stackpolebooks.com

Editor and text supervisor: journalist Thomas Vinge; subject adviser: Peter Tibert Stoltze; illustrations: Thomas Weiergang; photo: photographic journalist Tim K. Jensen

Other photos

Peter Tibert Stoltze: Page 56, 112, 160
Thomas Weiergang: Page 24, 34, 37, 67, 70, 74, 166, 175, 189
Henrik Mortensen: Page 35, 45, 47, 52, 54, 58, 59, 81, 97, 169, 177
Erik Kyrping: Page 186
Alejandro Martello: Page 5, 20, 38, 39, 42, 78, 96, 108, 120, 125, 142, 164, 167
Steen Ramsgaard: Page 77, 176
Layout and design Søren Flarup

Printed in China

First English-language edition

10 9 8 7 6 5 4 3 2 1

Library of Congress Cataloging-in-Publication Data
Mortensen, Henrik.
  Fly casting : Scandinavian style / Henrik Mortensen.—1st ed.
    p. cm.
  Includes index.
  ISBN-13: 978-0-8117-0509-7 (hardcover)
  ISBN-10: 0-8117-0509-9 (hardover)
  1. Fly casting I. Title.
  SH454.2M67 2010
  799.12'4—dc22
                          2008041294

The perfect cast is the one that hooks a fish.

Contents

Foreword

Way back in the dark ages (the late 1970s), when I started teaching fly casting at my dad's fly-fishing school in England, casting and fishing techniques were pretty traditional and fly line designs were very basic. You could get either a double-taper or a weight-forward line, and that was all. At the time, I also competed in tournament casting events, using tackle that you would never think of fishing with and particularly (because distance was the ultimate goal in some of the events) using shooting heads. Somehow, in those days in the UK, tournament casting and fishing never crossed paths. Sure, a few people started playing with shooting heads in the late 1970s for distance casting on lakes and reservoirs, but for general fly fishing, and in rivers especially, virtually nobody in the UK ever thought of using a shooting head.

My view on this started to change as I talked to casters from around the world and began hearing of a style of casting that was becoming popular in Scandinavian countries. This style of casting took as little work or effort as possible, using shooting heads, fine shooting lines, and long, long leaders. This style of casting was supposedly particularly effective with two-handed salmon rods and for making efficient direction changes and coping with obstructions behind. It sounded fascinating, but with no proponents of this style in the UK, nor in the US when I first moved there, I had little opportunity to find out more.

Then one day, many years ago, I was demonstrating Spey casting techniques at a winter fly-fishing show in Somerset, New Jersey. At that time there was not a huge interest in Spey casting in the US. Indeed, in those days spey casting was considered so un-mainstream that I had to demonstrate outside, on frozen ponds, and in bitter icy temperatures, while regular fly casting was demonstrated inside the warm halls, on custom-built (unfrozen) casting ponds. However, there were enough hardcore people intrigued by this style of casting who were willing to freeze in the pursuit of knowledge.

Amongst the crowd, I noticed a tall, slim man watching my demonstration, and his air of observation made it clear he knew a lot more about Spey casting than anyone else watching. When I had finished casting, he came up and we started talking. He introduced himself as Henrik Mortensen and explained that he was a Dane, that he worked for Loop, and that he taught fly casting.

Henrik had one of the Loop rods that he used to use with him at the Somerset show—a light and fast Loop Green rod—and he quickly strung the rod up and threw a few casts.

He had a shooting head set up on the rod, and demonstrated an extraordinarily relaxed, effortless casting style that produced loops as tight as a needle with phenomenal line speed. This was my first true introduction to the Scandinavian style of casting.

The more I talked to Henrik, the more I discovered that he really knew what he was talking about, and that he had an understanding of casting far deeper and far more technical than anyone I had ever met. What's more, he had a way of describing the casts that made me eager to hear more. Henrik was the first person to make me truly aware of the advantages of Spey casting with shooting heads. His patient education and inarguable logic made me see that Spey casting was so much more than casting long belly lines, and the lack of effort that he exuded in all his casting strokes made it pretty obvious that there were vast benefits in casting his way.

Over the years, I have followed Henrik's teachings on his incredible DVDs and at various fly casting shows and Spey claves in Denmark and the US. Whenever I find myself at a show where Henrik is casting, I always make a point of watching his demonstrations and listening to his explanations. Henrik demonstrates very clear and easy-to-follow instructions, combining the infinite patience of a seasoned fly casting instructor, a phenomenal grasp and understanding of just how fly casting works, and a clarity of communication that I have rarely seen.

The pages in this book are a natural extension of Henrik's films and demonstrations, and it is about time that the English-speaking world was treated to his written word. *Fly Casting Scandinavian Style* is one of those rare books that bridge the chasm between great instruction and awesome photography. The magnificent photos in this book are easily enough justification for anyone to buy a copy, but coupled with Henrik's easy-to-understand teachings and his clear instructive style, this book becomes an absolute must-have.

In short, any fly caster wishing to improve his casting technique should read this book. Whether a novice caster seeking to tighten a loop or take the first steps learning to double haul, or an accomplished caster aiming to develop a deep understanding of tackle and casting techniques, this book will certainly enhance and improve any caster's ability and knowledge base. And the photos? Well, they just make the reader want to journey in Henrik's shoes and fly-fish the world.

—Simon Gawesworth

Preface

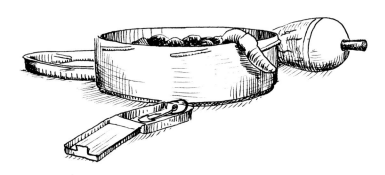

A cork bobber, a box of hooks, a can of freshly dug crawlers. The recipe for happiness can be that simple when you are a boy and a love of fishing has you firmly in its grasp. At least, that's the way it was for me. As long as I can remember, I've been driven by an inexplicable and overwhelming desire to go fishing.

My father, an engineer, took me fishing as soon as I was old enough to handle a rod. Sometimes he took me to creeks or nearby rivers; sometimes we hunted pike, perch, and roach in the local lakes. I was the sort of kid for whom the dinner hour, homework, and the phrase "clean up your room" were infinitely less important than a quick escape to the creek, pond, or pier.

Now that fly fishing is my profession, my thoughts often stray to those carefree expeditions with my rod in hand and my faithful dog at my side. What must have seemed an obsession to adults at the time was really a way for me to wrestle with some of life's finer challenges. Happily, these forays led me in a positive direction, due in no small part to a fortuitous encounter with a stranger on my creek. This chance meeting changed my life.

At the age of 12, I moved—along with my parents and two siblings—from Give in Central Jutland (Denmark) to the village of Hillerslev near Thisted in northern Jutland. We were newcomers, and fitting in and getting to know new classmates was tough work. We spoke a dialect that was viewed as more uptown than the native tongue, and we might just as well have been from a foreign country. I was young and did not understand, but we were different nonetheless.

Nearly everyone else lived on nearby farms and had chores to do in the afternoon. I did not live on a farm but in a detached house, and my afternoons were usually free. As there were few available playmates in the afternoon and my father was still at work when I returned from school, I went fishing whenever I could. My dad's and my shared interest in things with fins was not diminished by our change of address, however, and our spare time was filled with an activity that meant a great deal to us.

My older brother went along in the beginning, but his interest waned when he discovered that bikes (and later, mopeds) could be taken apart and, if he was lucky, reassembled. Buster, our German shepherd, shared my interest in wildlife and adventure. Buster was to become my best buddy and constant companion, and the streams and ponds within range of my bike were our boundless playground.

After school, I would toss my book bag into the far corner of the garage. Homework could stay there for all I cared. I swiftly tied my rod to the bike, grabbed the rest of my fishing gear, and whistled for Buster, who would quickly leap out of his enclosure. We were inseparable partners.

I suppose that some people may have thought that I was a little off my rocker. I spent all my free time down at the creek with Buster, and there was a complete lack of sympathy for my inability to remember mealtimes. But I took it all in stride, and in time my mother gave up trying to teach me normal routines. Somehow she came to terms with the fact that her boy was a little different when it came to fishing.

One fine fall day in 1973, I left for the creek after school as usual. It was a mile or so ride on the bike before Buster and I stood at the creek, which was actually a canal that drained water from the marshes. The canal was not completely straight: plenty of curves, aquatic plants, and weed beds provided shelter for trout.

When we reached the creek, I leaned my bike against the bridge in the usual fashion and walked along the water's edge with Buster in the lead. A half hour later, we reached our secret hole. I hardly ever saw a soul in my secret spot, so the sight of a grown man waving a strange rod back and forth in the air stopped me in my tracks. I was gutted. It was as if something sacred had been taken from me. I studied the trespasser from a distance. He sure had a funny way of casting a worm, and his line looked weird as well . . . like a piece of rope . . . and he cast it backward as well as forward.

The stranger noticed me. After a while, he came over, smiled, and said something unintelligible. I had no clue what he was saying. I couldn't figure out if I should run away or stick around and try to look tough. Sensing my indecision, Buster growled and bared his teeth. The man froze. It was obvious that he was frustrated by his inability to communicate his good intentions and a little intimidated by Buster.

I told Buster to be quiet and the man's smile returned. He carried on in his strange language and pointed eagerly to the worm on my hook. I looked on in wonder, and tried to pretend that I understood what he was talking about—he must be out of bait! I quickly found a can marked "Strawberry Preserves" in my jacket pocket and dug out a particularly fine pair of crawlers. The man made a strange face, and I immediately returned the worms to their recycled container.

The man went through his own pockets and removed something that looked like a tin lunchbox from his breast pocket. He opened the box and showed me its contents.

The box was filled with row upon row of tiny hooks with feathers and hairs tied on them. He neatly pulled a couple of these feathery concoctions from his box and handed them to me with a smile and a nod.

I really didn't know whether to accept the gift. The man gently took my fishing rod and clipped off the hook with a pair of nail scissors attached to a clever-looking contraption on his fishing vest. Instead of a bait hook, he attached one of the feathered hooks. He moved the bobber up the line a bit, returned the rod with a smile, uttered a friendly goodbye, and moved on down the creek.

I stared at the slowly disappearing figure for quite a while and then looked down at the feathered hook on the end of my line. It looked pretty, and I wondered if I could catch fish on such a strange thing. I dumped my fishing bag in the grass and tossed the new rig out into the current. The feathered hook was clearly visible as it drifted with the current beneath the bobber. I followed its progress for a while and grew impatient.

I decided to switch back to worms. As I started to retrieve the line, a wave suddenly appeared behind the bobber. A solid tug jerked the rod forward, and I had a fish on! Wow! After a short fight, I landed a nice brown trout just shy of 18 inches. Hmm. . . I guess you have to pull the feathered hook through the water to make the fish grab, I thought. I had to try that again.

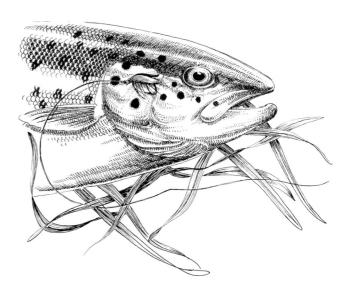

A bit farther down the creek was a bend that usually held a nice fish. I cast the bobber to the far bank, let it drift for a while, and then slowly started to retrieve the line. I spotted a flash in the water below the bobber and raised the rod. I had another trout on!

On my way down the creek I caught four more trout. My head was buzzing like a beehive. It was hard to fathom what I had just experienced. I shared my elation with Buster, and

I think I talked his ears off that day. I could barely wait for my next trip to town when I planned to buy some more of those feathered hooks at the local sports store. To think that I would never have to dig worms again! I never saw the man on the creek again. I often think of our chance encounter and his fine gesture. He opened my eyes to the world of trout on a fly.

After a couple of years I bought my first fly-fishing outfit—a Swedish rod from ABU in Svängsta, a fly line, and a smart triangular fly reel. From my days with the worm rod, I knew that I could find fish. And yet, it's a wonder that I became a die-hard fly fisherman: I often put my fly in the reeds, which towered above the banks along the embankment of the creek. I acquired a passable casting style and a high backcast to avoid the jungle behind me. There were no other fly fishermen around, so I was completely self-taught.

I soon began to explore the rest of the creek. I knew each and every bend, every outflow of current, and every rock or lie that might hold a trout. I soon discovered some unusually big trout farther down the slow-moving creek. When I came home with the first of these big brown trout, I was told that it was a sea trout. I borrowed a book on freshwater fish from the school library the very next day and went to work on the difference between sea trout and brown trout. It was without doubt the book that I studied more than any other during my school years.

It became a major obsession to find and fool these large fish in my local creek. Night fishing, which I had read about in fishing books, was out of the question due to the perilous casting conditions. I was forced to find the fish in the daytime. As the creek was very clear and quite shallow, conditions were demanding to say the least. There were three periods of the day when I stood a good chance of being successful: daybreak, sunset, and usually around noon on days when a

hard westerly wind combed the meadows. During these periods, both the sea trout and the usually demure brown trout would be active.

Traditional sea trout patterns were useless in the slow-moving creek. The Girdle Bug—usually a size 6 or a size 8—was my best fly pattern. I learned how to tie the fly from a fly-tying book. The Girdle Bug features a chenille body and three pairs of rubber legs sticking out from each side of the body. It's a strange looking rig. I would cast the fly far upstream, let it sink to the bottom, and make it rise to the surface by stripping in the line. If a fish followed the fly, I would speed up the retrieve: the faster the retrieve, the more violent the take. I used a relatively light 5-weight rod and had some memorable scraps with sea trout in the 5- to 10-pound range.

I caught my biggest sea trout in the creek when I was 15 or 16 years old. The fish measured 37 inches. I was alone when I caught it and in such a hurry to get home with my catch that I left my rod at the creek. It was one of the best days of my life.

I ventured farther and farther downstream until I reached the brackish waters of the Limfiord. I saw the occasional sea trout jumping way out in the fiord and figured that I could catch them in salt water. By my mid-twenties, I was chasing sea trout in the salt almost exclusively.

I could now fish for sea trout all year round. I soon met other anglers who shared my passion, many who were fly fishermen. Much of what I had learned on the creek also

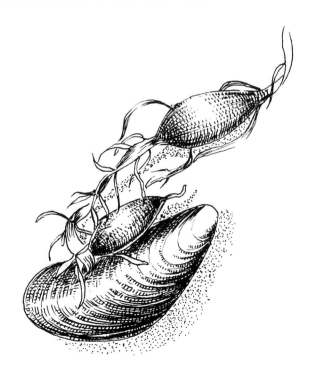

applied to the open ocean. I used the wind, for example, to my advantage. Long ago, I had discovered that I could sneak up close to fish on windy days. Wind creates waves, and sea trout are considerably more aggressive in a proper wave.

When I first started fly fishing from shore, I thought that I needed a sinking line. The sea is deep, or so I figured. I struggled to cast these sinking lines and to keep my fly from hanging up on the bottom. I switched to a floating line when I saw sea trout feeding on top and was far more successful from that point on.

I worked on my casting so that I could cover more water. I learned how to make long, smooth casts in order to cover the maximum amount of shoreline and give the fish just the right look at the fly. I soon discovered that sea trout in the salt were far less selective than the sea trout of the creek, and I tried to show my fly to as many fish as possible.

I was now fishing many of the local streams. One small, clear creek in particular became my favorite. The creek had a healthy supply of large brown trout. As these fish were actively feeding, it was important to match the hatch and to present the fly accurately with a smooth cast and a long line. These trout were considerably harder to fool than the sea trout that I caught from shore. Everything had to be just right; otherwise, you could forget about fooling these red-spotted beauties.

I started teaching casting technique and fishing strategy at the age of 26. I ran two fishing courses for youngsters as part of my first official duties. After four winters of teaching, I applied to be an instructor in the Danish Angling Association. The selection committee comprised two instructors from the angling association. As part of the test, I taught a weeklong course for aspiring, young outdoor leaders from all over Denmark. The Danish Angling Association works to create better conditions for both fish and fishermen, and I was proud to help them to achieve their goals.

One of my first official duties as an instructor for the Danish Angling Association took place on Sealand, the central island of Denmark, at a country game fair. I stood in a punt in the middle of a lake. While I cast (and tried to keep my balance), my friend Steffen Juhl, microphone in hand, walked the bank and explained my every move to the crowd with the practiced delivery of a sports commentator. The bar had been raised. I was no longer casting just for fun but to show how the cast is made and how to avoid the most common mistakes.

The event was the first fly-casting demonstration hosted by the Danish Angling Association for the general public. It was a great success, and over the years, I have participated in many similar demonstrations. Working for the Danish Angling Association was an important part of my development as an instructor. Teaching gives me great personal satisfaction and joy, and it is always rewarding to share my passion for angling with students who love the sport as much as I do.

And with that, I moved away from my years of isolation as an angler. I learned a great deal from other exceptional instructors and anglers. Among the many great friends that I made through the years, Peter Stoltze stands out in particular. Peter and I were on the same wavelength from day one, and we toured the country for many years, giving courses on casting technique and fishing strategy.

A year or so before I became an instructor in the Danish Angling Association, I took a class from Göran Andersson, "the wizard from Gävle." Göran developed a cast he called the underhand cast and was ahead of his time in many respects. Göran's mastery of the fly rod has inspired many to take up the sport. I found it easy to cast the way Göran wanted his students to cast. It was, in fact, the way I had taught myself to cast on my own creek: an early stop on the backcast, a short drift, and a smooth forward stroke with a high rod stop. I was not aware why my casting went so smoothly, but Göran put words to it.

In 1993, I attended another of Göran's courses in Denmark. Göran invited me to participate in one of his double-handed casting classes on the Orkla River in Norway. Soon thereafter, I started work with Loop Tackle, a company that Göran cofounded in 1984. The first couple of years, I tested tackle and held courses in casting technique; it soon turned into a full-time job. Although I worked at Loop for ten years—through 2002—Göran and I hardly ever saw each other. We were in contact on the phone a couple of times a year, but we never fished or held classes together. Göran concentrated on rod development, while I focused on the development of fly lines, leaders, and fly-fishing accessories.

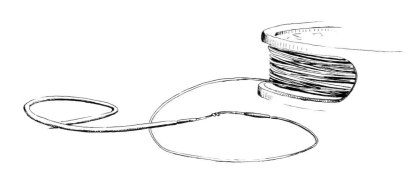

I was the driving force behind the Loop Adapted Line System. Up until that point, most anglers used double-taper lines or standard weight-forward lines. Shooting heads were very popular for tournament distance casting but lacked the necessary delicacy for practical fishing.

The new Adapted Line System used a modular approach to simplify the fly-fishing experience. Each module had its own color: the shooting line had one color, and each shooting head had a different color depending on its sink rate. Color-coded factory loops denoted different line sizes. Polyleaders with different sink rates maximized presentation and allowed the angler to fish the fly at exactly the right depth. I worked closely with Airflo, the manufacturer of the line in the UK, to make sure everything was just right. Loop marketed the Adapted Line System and released the product at a time when interest in two-handed casting had never been greater.

I also held salmon schools in Norway and in England and performed casting demonstrations at major angling fairs. I

taught scores of classes on casting technique and fishing strategy at tackle shops in Denmark and Sweden. I usually averaged between 800 and 1,400 participants each year in locations as diverse as the United States, Canada, Korea, Italy, Germany, England, Iceland, Norway, Sweden, and Denmark.

Iceland has been my summer home since 1995. I give casting instruction and conduct guiding and fishing seminars on many of the country's spectacular salmon rivers (there are 96 rivers in total). I started with casting classes and demonstrations arranged by a couple of tackle shops in Reykjavik. I soon met Arni Baldursson from Angling Club Laxá, who leases many of the finest salmon rivers in Iceland. Arni asked me to come back the following season to provide supplementary training for his guides in fly casting, fishing strategy and tactics, and streamside etiquette.

I also worked as a guide in Iceland for the next five seasons. It was really hard work. Each day began with the sun and ended at dark. Days off were nonexistent. I observed salmon and sea trout behavior from the first push of fish in June right through the final runs of the season in September and October. I saw again and again the importance of the correct fishing strategy and proper casting technique. The fly must fish efficiently from the moment it hits the water until the moment it leaves the water for the next cast. I also learned

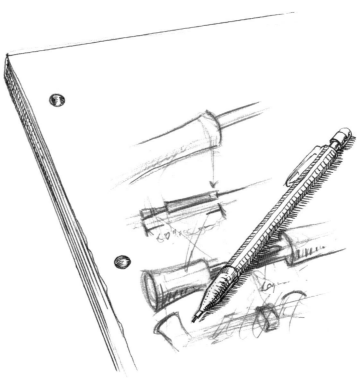

how important it is to have good gear when you're on the river all day.

Having been fortunate to make my avocation my vocation, I eventually earned enough credibility to land an amazing job as the head of design and development for Scierra, a division of Svendsen Sport, creating groundbreaking new products. After nearly six years with Scierra, in summer of 2008, I joined Zpey Systems, a unique Scandinavian fly-fishing company, as the head of research and development. We are currently building the company into what I believe will be a worldwide leader in the fly-fishing industry. It is fun and challenging to design and develop rods, lines, and fly-fishing accessories for the discriminating angler! We are developing a finely tuned network of manufacturers located all over the world. This diversity provides unique advantages when developing new products. It's a lot of fun to take a wild idea from the drawing board right through to its product launch. But it's even more rewarding to see the gear being used successfully on the river.

Most fishing tackle is manufactured in the Far East these days, and I visit several manufacturers in Asia each winter. Product development takes place during the winter at my residence in the United States. Product development is really a year-round activity, but I use these winter months to bring shape to ideas that I have on the water or receive through my interaction with the many anglers that I meet each year.

I test new products during the spring and summer months. I'm happy to report that being indoors is of no use for this enterprise! There's no way around it—it takes a lot of casting and fishing.

As a boy, the fishing rod and the outdoors were my friends of choice. They still are to this day! I have a fly rod in my hand more than 290 days a year, and I travel to all corners of the world to teach fly casting and fly fishing. It is extremely rewarding to share my passion for fly fishing with students who love the sport as much as I do.

And now I have penned this book, which I sincerely hope will help you become a better fly caster. May you experience again and again the satisfaction of the perfect cast—the one that catches a fish!

Tight lines,

Henrik Mortensen

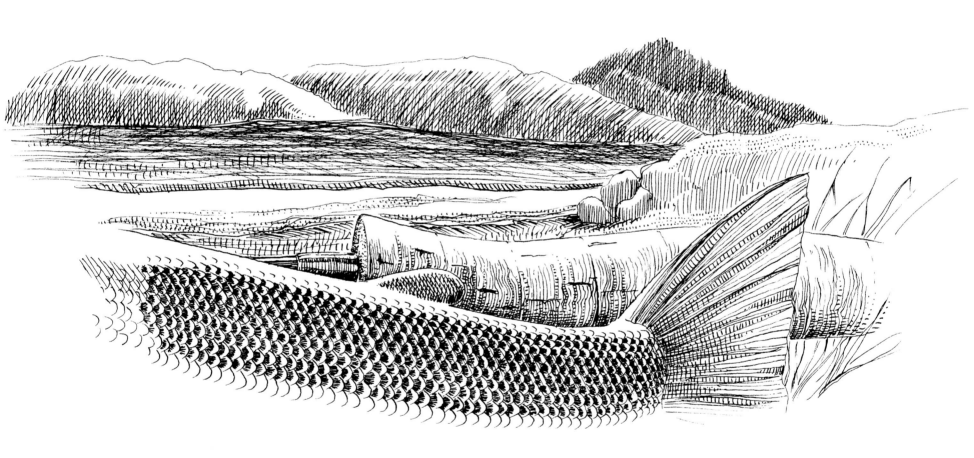

Introduction

A moment in life. Irigoyen, Tierra del Fuego.

There are already several fine books on fly casting on the market, so why write another one on the subject? The answer is quite simple, really: because there is a need for one. New generations of rods and lines have seen the light of day in the last few years and they have added new dimensions to what is possible within fly casting. Natural conditions such as wind and gravity are unchanged, but because of the ever-improving fly fishing tackle, you can do casts today that were impossible 15–20 years ago. Hence the need for the book you have in your hand.

This book is based on my own experience as a guide and instructor of fly casting and fishing strategy all over the world. Throughout the years, I have taught many thousands of fly fishers and have met all types of anglers—beginners all well as seasoned guides. I would like to pass on what is, in my experience, the perfect cast with a fly.

This means that the book is all about *my* way to cast a fly and *my* conception of the essentials of fly casting with single- and double-handed rods.

My wish is that the combination of text, color photographs, and illustrations in this book will make it easier for the beginner to really understand the cast from the start.

If you would like to learn how to cast a fly and only have little experience, I would recommend that you start with chapters 3 and 4. They deal with tackle composition and the basic technique of the overhead cast.

In addition, I recommend that you join a casting course with an experienced instructor. He or she will immediately see the weak spots in your cast and correct whatever faults you may have before they become nasty habits. You will get an explanation to a lot of the special terms that crowd any fly fisher's vocabulary.

If you're already an experienced caster, I hope that the reading will bring you many eye-openers and a deeper under- standing of the mechanical actions and possibilities of the fly cast, as well as inspiration to set new goals for your fishing.

I have read many books on casting technique but have often missed a more detailed account of the fly cast's composition and how to put together the fly gear optimally. In fact, details often determine whether a cast is successful or not. That's why I make an effort to describe how to hold the rod properly, for example, or how the rod is passed back and forth between the different positions in the cast. I also talk about the leader's importance in the cast. These details are important if you want to keep a check on the casting. Only when you control the cast will you be able to concentrate fully on the fishing.

A fly cast that does not have as its goal to get the fly to fish in the best possible way has no legitimacy in my opinion. For this reason, I put a great deal of emphasis on the composition of tackle, so that I can control my cast, deliver and fish the fly, and not have to take into consideration whether there's any room for a backcast or not.

The content of this book is at times quite technical. It is not a book to read from cover to cover. Instead, I would recommend that you read it slowly and thoroughly and spend some time after each chapter on the practical side of things in order to gain a better understanding of the content before you move on.

It is my wish and goal that all who read this book will have the best chances to develop and perfect their casting—not for the sake of the cast itself, but to contribute to their fishing with the joy that they experience when the cast is running smoothly and the fly lands exactly where they want it, each time!

Enjoy your read.

Chapter 1
The Physics of the Fly Cast

Once you understand the mechanical actions of the fly cast, surroundings will no longer dictate your choice of water.
Petit Cascapédia, Canada.

The fly caster's signature

If you were to sum up what the modern fly caster is striving for, it can be done in two words: good-looking loops! Being a skilled fly caster has a certain status attached to it, and good-looking loops are the signature of the skilled fly caster. So what is a good-looking loop? In my opinion, it is a loop that is controlled 100 percent. It may appear in different shapes, but the hallmark is a cast controlled completely by the fly caster.

In order to constantly deliver controlled loops, you must understand the basic physical principles of the fly cast. You'll find that the fishing will be better and more interesting if you sit down and think the cast through in any given situation: how should the fly be placed in order to get the right movement over a possible holding area?

Take salmon fishing with a fly skating the surface, called riffling hitch, as an example (see pages 34–37). Here you have a situation where it is of the utmost importance that the fly fishes from the moment it touches water and rides the surface throughout the drift. But if you use a standard-length leader, the current will grab the fly and drown it. The solution is to use a leader that is, theoretically, far too short.

If you think the cast through, you'll realize that the fly line, as a consequence of the short leader, will travel too fast, making the leader stretch too abruptly. The result will be either that the leader bounces back like a spring, which means that the fly will not fish before the current stretches the leader, or that the fly and leader hit the water with a splash, scaring the fish. To compensate, you must moderate and soften the cast before the fly touches the water.

Take a walk before the first cast

The standard casts described in this book cover most practical fishing situations. Once you thoroughly understand the mechanical actions behind every cast, you will be able to come up with variations that you can use during other situations. In fact, before you even present your fly on a demanding stream, you should have a plan of action as to how you will let the fly search the water.

I have made it a habit to spend some time scanning the stream before I wet the fly—and the same goes, of course, for a lake or coastal waters. I'd suggest that you do the same. Take a walk along the water and try to estimate depth and underwater structures. Make a mental note of places with a hard current and places where the current loses speed. Your observations will give you an indication of holding areas and about what size and pattern of fly is best suited for the water. Then choose a line and leader to suit the pattern and size of the fly. Decide whether the line and leader need to be floating, intermediate, or sinking, but only after you know where the fly is going to be presented to the fish: near the surface, in midwater, or near the bottom.

Plan ahead

After your reconnaissance, plan when and how to fish the different stretches of water. I pay particular attention to the sun's position and will make an effort to avoid having the sun behind me while I fish. Shadows thrown into the water by the fly fisherman and the rod, line, and leader may scare the fish.

Another aspect that I try to assess is where the fish may have its holding spots during the day. Many people believe that a fish will stick to a single holding spot until it decides to move farther upstream. I have a different view. I often see how salmon and sea trout move around depending on the sun's position, making me believe that you have to be ready to seize an opportunity—and the most opportune time to fish a holding area is when a fish has just taken its spot. Right then, the fish is active and easy to fool.

Now you can decide on the details of your fishing plan. It's all about trying to figure out how to fish the fly depending on different holding spots. Maybe you have places you need to wade into; in other places you may need to crawl on your hands and knees to fish a bank-side current without spooking the fish.

This is where a good casting technique comes into the picture. With an understanding of how the fly cast is structured and performed, you will be at liberty to cast from every possible and impossible angle and position. Undoubtedly, the time spent building up your casting skills will land you more fish and give you greater pleasure doing so. It is your reward for hanging in there with the carbon-flexing on the lawn!

Something about physics

The fly cast is on the one hand really simple and on the other very complex. It seems simple when a skilled fly caster sends the line flying in a precise and coordinated movement, but it becomes complex when physicists try to describe the fly cast quantitatively with simulations on a computer screen. They are getting quite good at that, but they still have a long way to go from the sketchy animations on the screen to the beauty that characterizes the cast made by a skilled fly caster.

To explain the cast graphically, you could say that a fly cast consists of a very long weight (the fly line) being moved by a flexible lever (the fly rod). We push and pull one end of the lever, flexing and unflexing it against the weight attached to the other end. The purpose of the pushing and pulling is to put the long weight into the desired final position.

Through training and practical fishing, the caster is, consciously or unconsciously, gradually able to master the interaction between lever and weight (fly rod and fly line). In the end, this interaction is what gives you nicely controlled loops.

The rod is loaded with energy

What we call flexing and unflexing the lever is also called "loading and unloading the blank." When the fly rod is completely straightened out, it is in its neutral position. To bend it from this neutral position demands energy. The greater part of this energy is stored in the blank as potential energy, which is also called gravitational potential energy. The more the rod bends (up to a critical point), the more energy is stored in it; hence the phrase "loading the rod."

When the rod is straightened out, it delivers the potential energy and the rod unloads. The more the rod has been bent, the more energy is delivered when it straightens out and the more power and speed transfer to the fly line.

The energy is delivered to the line in the form of kinetic energy, also known as energy of motion. The mass of kinetic energy in the line is found in the following formula:

$$\text{Kinetic energy} = \tfrac{1}{2} \times \text{mass} \times \text{speed}^2$$

Basically, a body with a given mass and a given speed contains a certain amount of kinetic energy.

It is tempting to think that the heavier the line is, the longer it can cast, but that is not the case. If two fly lines move with the same speed, but one of them is double the weight of the other, the heavier line will also hold twice the amount of kinetic energy in store. On the other hand, if two fly lines have the same weight but one is moving twice as fast as the other, the fastest line holds four times the amount of kinetic energy. So in practical fishing, the trick is to squeeze as much kinetic energy into the fly line as possible. The easiest way to do that is by giving it a lot of speed. The higher the speed of the fly line, the more energy it holds. In theory, it is easier to achieve a high speed with a smaller weight than with a heavier one. But in fly casting, if the line is too light, the wind may take it, making it hard to load the blank. Line design is therefore always a compromise between extremes.

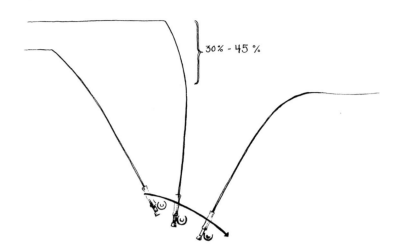

Do not push the rod forward and down when casting.

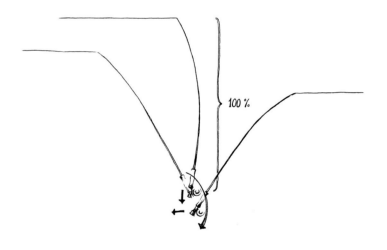

Figure 1-1. By moving the rod down and pulling it toward you, kinetic energy is loaded deeper in the blank.

Pulling or pushing?

A fly can be cast two basic ways: You can either *pull* the rod, or you can *push* the rod. In figure 1-1 we show two fundamentally different ways to affect the rod during a regular overhead cast. Above, the handle is *pushed* in an inclined movement forward and downward, while the lower drawing shows a downward *pull* of the handle.

The most efficient fly cast is, without doubt, achieved by *pulling* the handle down and toward you. This motion bends the blank deeply toward the cork handle, storing a considerable amount of potential energy. This potential energy is later transferred to the line in the form of speed.

If you only push the handle of the rod forward and down during the cast, you bend only the tip of the rod, storing less energy in the blank. The tip of the blank has a tendency to bend a lot when it is pushed in this way and, therefore, moves very fast. You can hear this movement as a swishing sound during the cast. This sound is a signal to you that your cast is not working as well as it could. Not only is the rod is not loading deeply because of the fast rod handling, your cast also loses precision.

When you pull the rod, however, the whole blank is flexed, or loaded, in one single, steady movement, and you will notice the absence of the swishing sound. The advantage of pulling and flexing the rod and blank deeper is that you get a calmer movement, making it easier to present the leader and fly precisely. In short you achieve better control over your cast.

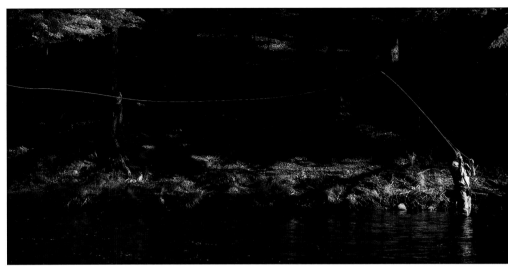

Figure 1-2. The rod is in the back position and the line is stretched out behind the caster.

The movement of the rod in the cast

Before the line is lifted from the water for a new cast, the fly fisherman is in the starting position with the rod lowered, pointing in the direction of the line straight on the water (or on the grass when you dry cast). The cast itself consists of four movements, described in the box below.

Analysis of the fly cast

As we begin our analysis of the make-up of a fly cast, our starting point is a fly line hanging straight back from the tip guide, as shown in figure 1-2. In the picture, the rod is in the position called the back position (see chapter 4 for more on this position).

---

1. **The lift:** *From the starting position, the caster moves the rod slowly and steadily backward to the front stop, pulling the line up and back, lifting it clear of the water, leaving the leader still attached to the surface.*
2. **The backcast.** *The rod is then moved in a steady acceleration from the front stop to the back stop where the speed is decreased considerably but without stopping the movement completely. At this point the loop builds up behind the caster.*
3. **The drift.** *This is a controlled lift in preparation of the forward cast, which starts the moment the line is straight. The caster lifts the elbow slightly forward and upward after the back stop, in a steady and quite slow movement. This causes the rod tip to move farther backward. The rod is now in the back position.*
4. **The forward cast.** *The caster finishes by keeping the angle between the upper arm and under arm closed, and by pulling the elbow back again until the rod reaches the front position. When the rod stops in the front position, the line is delivered over the water. At the point where the line is almost straight, the angle between the upper arm and forearm is opened, and the rod is lowered gradually as the line descends toward the water.*

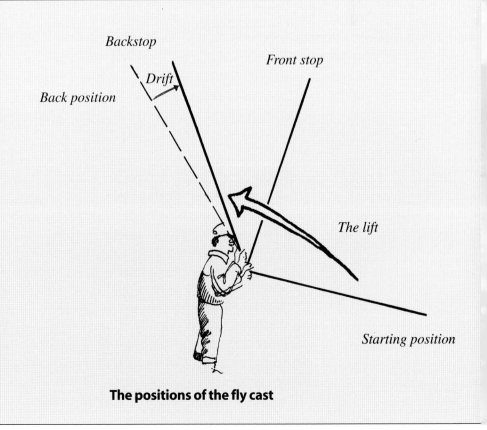

The positions of the fly cast

When the line is stretched behind you, move the rod forward toward the front stop. Remember, do not open the angle between upper arm and forearm. Instead, pull the locked elbow down and backward, until the rod is in the front stop. The line follows the pull from the tip guide, and shortly after, the line will be hanging in the air in a nice loop, more or less like the one seen in figure 1-3, which shows the basic terminology of fly casting.

Figure 1-3. The line can be divided into three parts: the upper line, the loop, and the lower line.

The upper line and the lower line are more or less parallel, while the loop describes a semicircle. In figure 1-4, the semicircle of the loop is shown with an imaginary wheel. The wheel illustrates the line displacements that occur during the cast.

If the upper line moves forward with a greater speed than the lower line, the wheel will turn clockwise (as shown in figure 1-4). The greater the difference of speed between the upper and lower line is, the greater the wheel's rotation speed. Notice that the wheel's rotation speed is not dependent on the actual speed of the upper and lower lines but on the difference between the two. The displacement speed of the wheel, however, follows the speed of the fastest part of the line (the upper line or the lower line). You need to have greater speed on the upper line; otherwise, the wheel will not turn forward. The cast will then collapse without stretching the leader.

With these concepts in mind, you could say that a controlled loop is a matter of handling the velocities of the wheel: speed of displacement and rotation speed. If you want to make long casts, you'll need to achieve a very high speed of displacement, which means a high velocity of both the upper and lower line. But at the same time, you need a slow rotational speed, giving the upper line slightly more speed than the lower line. Remember that as long as a loop is rolling forward, you can shoot line. When the wheel is slowly rotating, you will be able to shoot line for a longer period. (More about long-distance casting is found on pages 94–95.)

The forward cast in steps

The following series of drawings illustrates how the speed of displacement and rotation progress throughout the final forward cast. In order to help you better understand the dynamics of the cast, actual values of speed are listed on the drawings.

These values are hypothetical. The important things to note are the differences between the speed of the upper line, the loop, and the lower line. The difference between the speed of the upper line and the lower line equals the speed at which the loop moves through the air.

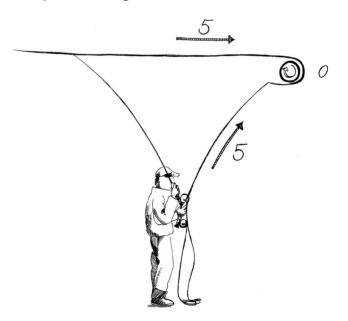

Figure 1-4.

On the illustration above, the upper line moves forward with a speed of 5. The caster has just released the running line and the speed of the lower line is the same as the starting speed of the upper line. This means that the lower line also moves with a speed of 5. The wheel has just been formed and is about to rotate.

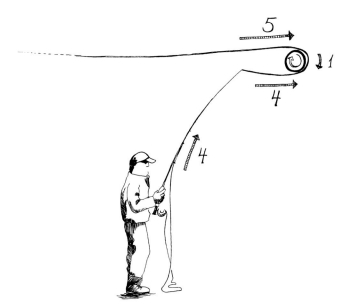

Figure 1-5.

In figure 1-5, the lower line is giving more resistance as a consequence of the line running out. When the line is shot out, the length of the lower line is increased and so is the resistance this length of line represents in the cast.

The added resistance means that the speed of the lower line has dropped to 4. But because the speed of the upper line is still at 5, the wheel is still rolling forward with a speed of 1, the difference between the speeds of the upper and lower lines.

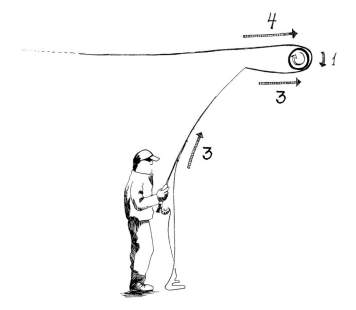

Figure 1-6.

As the energy of the cast decreases, the velocity of the upper and lower lines decreases.

In figure 1-6, the speed of the upper line has dropped to 4. As the running line glides through the guides, the lower line gets longer and longer, increasing the resistance on the lower line. This resistance means that the speed of the lower line drops.

But there is still a difference between the upper and lower lines. The wheel holds its speed, which is 1.

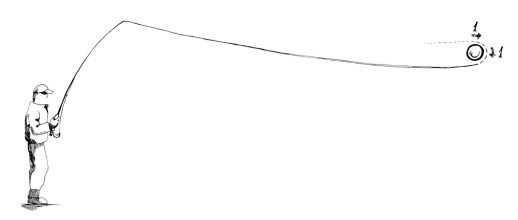

Figure 1-7.

In figure 1-7, the speed of the upper line has dropped almost completely, but the energy of the forward cast has been adjusted to the tackle; the lower line is no longer extended and has dropped to a speed of 0. In practice, this drop means that the last energy of the upper line is used to stretch the leader. A well-executed fly cast depends on a stretched leader.

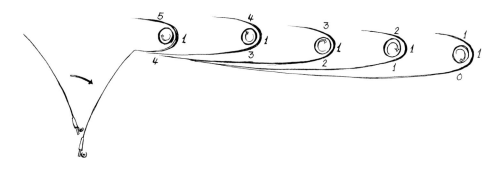

Figure 1-8.

Figure 8 shows the development of the fly cast presented in sequence. A cast is controlled and successful when the relations between the velocities of the line parts are as described above.

These velocities are governed by the way in which the fly tackle is composed. (Read more about this in chapter 3.)

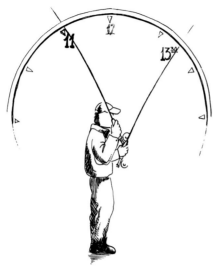

The face of a watch is often used to show the casting angle from eleven o'clock to half past one.

The direction of the cast and the size of the loop

For many years, the fly cast has been described as a movement between eleven and half past one on the face of a clock, as shown in figure 1-8. This simplified version of the cast is not quite correct. For instance, using the face of a clock to explain the cast does not tell how the loop is made. The development is best described based on the following two rules:

> **1.** *In the forward cast, the loop is made as a consequence of the height difference between the back position and the tip guide in the front stop. Line position also plays a major part in forming the loop in the backcast.*
> **2.** *The development of the loop and the direction of the forward cast are results of the position of the line in the backcast.*

For example, the line could descend behind the caster, giving it an inclined angle in the forward cast, which will result in a large loop (see figure 1-11). The line could also hang almost horizontally behind the caster in the backcast, giving a tight loop in the forward cast (see figure 1-10).

The same rules apply for the backcast. In this instance, however, the difference between the front stop and the back stop, and the position of the line in lift, decide the outcome.

So the direction of the line in the forward cast—and how big the loop is going to be—is already decided in the backcast because the position of the first third of the line behind

the tip guide determines the direction of the cast and the size of the loop. This rule not only applies to the overhead cast, but also for casts from the water, which includes the roll cast and Spey cast. The following drawings of overhead casts illustrate these rules.

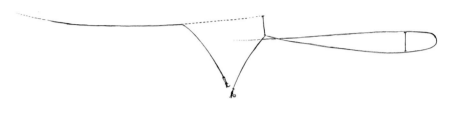

Figure 1-9.

Figure 1-9 shows a relatively short cast where the tip guide in the back position is a little higher than the tip guide in the front stop, which means that an ever so slight *drift* has been made. The drift appears when you lift your elbow slightly forward and up after the back stop; as a consequence the rod tip goes farther backward. The size of the loop is determined by the difference in height between the tip at the back position and the front stop.

Notice also that the upper line toward the end of the forward cast is actually below the tip guide. It is therefore important that the angler never move the rod forward and backward in a completely horizontal plane, because both the upper and lower line will descend due to gravity and the line will be prone to collide with the rod tip in the front stop. Instead, angle the rod out a bit when it is moved backward and forward.

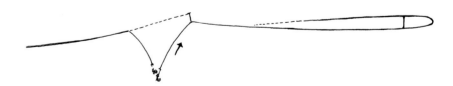

Figure 1-10.

Figure 1-10 shows a cast with a longer line and a deeper drift. Seen along a horizontal plane, the tip guide in the back position is below the tip guide in the front stop, which gives the line an upside down loop where the end of the fly line and the leader create the lower line.

But theory holds that the tip's height difference decides the size of the loop. So, in a long cast, such as the one shown in

A narrow and high-flying line loop can go a long way.

the drawing, the line will drop down a bit in the back position. It takes longer to stretch a long line, and for that period of time, the fly line descends toward the ground, which makes the line hang lower than normal in the beginning of the backcast. In other words, the line will, toward the end of the backcast, fall below the level of the tip guide until the loop has rolled out completely, making the forward cast shoot slightly upward and creating the height difference between the tip at the back position and the front stop, which determines the height of the loop.

Figure 1-11.

The position of the line in the backcast

In figure 1-11, the back position and the front stop are similar to those in figure 1-9, but the casts on these two drawings are far from identical because the line position at the completion of the backcast is different. In figure 1-9, the line is hangs horizontally behind the caster in the backcast; in figure 1-11, it hangs lower. In most cases, this happens when you lift the line, before the backcast is initiated, but in figure 1-11, the line hangs lower because you hesitated too long after the line has stretched out in the air behind you. As you hesitate,

the line descends behind you, and when you finally start the forward cast, the line will travel skyward in a steep incline, resulting in a large loop. In most cases, this is a disadvantage because an open loop is more sensitive to the wind than a tight loop. An open loop also takes more energy to deliver in the forward cast, and therefore, you tend to lose both control and precision. Remember that the rod's stop positions and the placement of the line in the backcast are interconnected concepts. Understanding the way the line is delivered in the backcast has a great deal of influence on both direction and loop size in the forward cast.

A good cast starts with a good lift

The lift on the backcast is an essential yet overlooked part of a well-made fly cast. A good start goes half the way, according to an old Danish saying, and the same goes for fly casting. A well-performed lift will give you a good backcast, which in turn is the basis for a good forward cast.

The lift also decides the placement of the line in the backcast and, ultimately, where the forward cast ends. The better you can place your line in the backcast, the more variations of the forward cast you will be able to achieve. This is why I pay such close attention to this part of the cast in this book.

The length of the line belly

In order to make a good lift, the line's belly must be adjusted to fit the rod. Most tackle manufacturers design lines with promising names such as Long Distance and Long Spey. Generally speaking, these lines have rather long and heavy bellies, and advertising experts have apparently claimed that long, heavy bellies will give you a long cast. Documentation backing these claims is rare, however, and there is good reason for that.

Many anglers adapt their own lines by cutting a double-taper line in half, and then they keep on cutting until the belly suits their purpose. By doing so, they end up with a shooting head or a belly in an attempt to hit the right weight. The result is, more often than not, a length of line cut more or less randomly.

I am convinced that you have to leave the question of weight out of the picture from the start because *length* is ultimately more important than *weight* in a fly cast. Why? You have to cast a certain amount of line to be able to make a loop that will work for you. If the shooting head is too short, you will have problems executing longer casts, and you will also find it hard to build up the dynamic energy that, especially toward the end of the cast, is necessary to stretch the leader. Instead, the leader will land in a pile and the fly won't start fishing until the current has stretched the leader, or until the angler has stripped the line to pick up the loose leader. Neither option is any good.

Long or short, the belly has to fit your rod
Figures 1-12, 1-13, and 1-14 show how the line is placed in the backcast depending on the length of the belly.

A very short belly makes it hard to lift the line properly, but a very long belly does, too. The result is a poor backcast with a wide angle and a large loop, which leads to a sloppy forward cast and poor presentation of the fly. If, that is, the fly ever gets that far: The loop in the backcast often takes the fly down to ground level, where a tuft of grass, a tree, or a bush can get a hold of it. Or the fly may hit a rock, breaking off the hook point. A belly that is too long can also mean that you have to do more false casting, which is tiring and disturbs the water unnecessarily. Remember, the less false casting you do, the more time you have to fish the fly effectively.

When you have fished the cast through, you have to decide where you want the fly to land for the next cast. By thinking ahead, you'll know how to perform the lift to make the fly line sail backward in the exact line of where you want your forward cast to go. You may have to do a roll cast, where the line is rolled up to angle it into the desired direction before the lift. The roll cast also results in less false casting and fewer spooked fish.

A suitable belly
Figure 1-12 shows a cast with a suitable belly. Here you have an acceptable flat angle in the front stop between the line and the surface, which consequently results in a flat backcast. The trick is to throw the line backward at an angle that is close to the angle you want it to have in the forward cast. If the line is thrown back too high, you will probably see the line splashing into the water in the forward cast. If the line is thrown back too low, you may end up hooked in trees or bushes during the backcast.

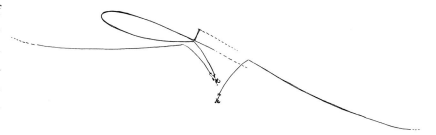

Figure 1-12.

Beautiful, tight loops
The loop itself can be tight or open. Most often, your goal should be to create a tight loop, which has less wind resistance and greater speed.

In several situations, though, you may need an open loop. For example, if you have the wind at your back, the wind will then help to roll over an open loop, while a tight loop may gather too much speed, making the fly splash on impact. Dry-fly fishers should employ soft, relatively open loops because open loops make for more precision when the fly is delivered. The same goes for salmon fishing on a short line, where an open loop will help you present the fly exactly in the right eddy or some other small holding spot.

The ideal loop
The size of the loop in the backcast is determined by the rod tip's height difference at the front stop and the back stop, and the placement of the line after the completion of the lift and before the acceleration is initiated. In figure 1-12, the loop is ideal in size and shape. The result is the perfect backcast, which affords the caster optimal conditions to execute a controlled forward cast and a good presentation of the fly.

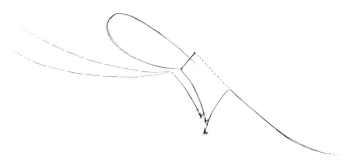

Figure 1-13.

In figure 1-13, the shooting head is too short. You may see this type of cast among casters who cut their own shooting heads to get a specific weight. It may seem like a good idea to choose an ultra-short belly for fishing in places with trees or big bushes along the water's edge, or in rivers where a steep bank or wall of rock hinders a normal backcast. Many anglers make ultra-short shooting heads for such cramped conditions. Instead of a normal belly of 10 to 12 meters, they cut their lines, resulting in bellies of maybe half that length. During the front stop, the angle between the line and the surface is rather steep, and because the front stop and back stop positions haven't changed, a big loop appears in the backcast. In practice, it is hard to change the front stop or back stop to make a decent cast with a line this short. In addition, the line is directed in a steep angle upward, meaning that it will hang in a great bow, without stretching out behind the caster before the forward cast is initiated. The result is a big and uncontrollable loop in the forward cast.

Troubles with short bellies
Short bellies are rarely suitable for either casting or fishing because the weight is carried on a short piece of line, making the cast hard to control. The calm and dynamic balance disappears: either the back end of the belly lands first because of the weight or the leader won't stretch properly. In short, the line is out of control and chance decides where and how the fly lands.

Making lines exclusively for places with little elbowroom is generally not advisable. Instead you should adjust the casting movements and cast with a shorter line outside the tip guide in places like these. In fact, it is possible, with a well-chosen all-around line and a fly rod with the right action, to handle almost any kind of situation without having to change your line. A rod with the right action performs with any line length outside the tip guide.

Long bellies are hard to handle

In figure 1-14, the caster is trying to cast with a shooting head that is much too long. It could be a so-called long belly line, a traditional Spey line, or just a regular belly.

The result is that the line descends too far in the backcast before it stretches out. This dip means that the leader and the tip of the line can easily become tangled up in bushes and trees during the backcast. The low starting point of the line in the backcast also results in a large and uncontrollable loop in the forward cast.

The real reason why this cast is not working is that controlled lifts are difficult to accomplish with the long and heavy line, and that is why a good backcast is hard to achieve.

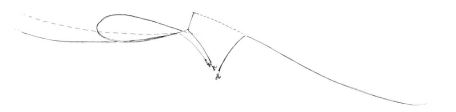

Figure 1-14.

A long belly takes perfect timing
Traditional Spey lines can perform very well with a Spey cast or an overhead cast, but they take up too much room because the casting weight is spread out over a long piece of line. Precise timing of the cast becomes crucial.

You will need to invest a great deal of energy to give speed to a long and heavy line. Add a sinking line on top of that, and casting takes even more muscle.

If you do succeed in getting the long, heavy line flying, the line will in fact contain enough energy to cast a long way. But even a skilled fly fisher does not time his Spey cast perfectly every single time, and with this kind of line, the cast can easily get out of hand if the timing is not right.

I have never seen, anywhere in the world, on any of my travels, a fly fisher who could easily and leisurely cast a whole long-belly Spey line, either by using a Spey cast or an overhead cast. Usually the cast is made with a vigorous display of muscle.

Hitching, the closest thing to heaven with a fly rod

Hitching on the banks of Petit Cascapédia in Gaspe, Canada.

Hitching—waking a wet fly across the surface of a river—has captivated me for more than ten years. The more I hitch, the more I become hooked on the technique. The best part about hitching is that you not only feel the take of the salmon, but you also see the fish break the surface of the water as it takes your fly.

Fishing for Atlantic salmon with the riffling hitch has its roots in Canada. In his groundbreaking work *The Atlantic Salmon*, Lee Wulff describes how he was introduced to the method during a trip to Portland Creek in Newfoundland.

The local guides used the technique almost exclusively and claimed that it was the only way to catch a salmon in their river. Wulff was skeptical and wondered if the standard wet-

fly swing was, in fact, receiving a fair shake. Wulff fished several of the best holding spots with standard wet flies without any success.

Things got interesting when he tied on a size 8 Jock Scott. As the fly fished across the current, the knot in his leader created a tiny V-shaped wake on the surface. Ignoring his fly, a salmon rose up and hit the knot on the leader. With this experience fresh in his mind, Wulff could see no good reason why a salmon would not take a fly behaving in the same manner.

Wulff soon tied on a fly using the knot the guides had shown him so that the fly would skate on the surface. The knot caused the fly to wake in the surface layer of the current

This micro tube has a hole in the side where the leader is inserted to make it hitch.

A 2½-inch sunray shadow hitch with a clove knot to make it hitch.

as it fished its way across the river. A salmon took it on the second cast!

Wulff did not invent the riffling hitch, but he certainly popularized the technique through his articles and books. The genesis of the riffling hitch goes way back in time. In the mid-nineteenth century, English ships often anchored near the mouth of Portland Creek, and the officers on board went ashore to fish. The flies of the day were tied on hooks without a metal eye: in contrast to today's ring-eye or return-wire hooks, these blind-eye hooks used a loop of gut to form the eye of the hook. The locals got their hands on some of the English flies, but over time the gut eyes became worn or broken. The local anglers secured the damaged flies with a couple of half hitches right behind the head of the fly and fished them anyway. The fly waked across the surface of the water with this new point of attachment; the rest, as they say, is history.

Active stripping

I hitched my first fly in the summer of 1995 in Iceland, and I have since experimented with the technique for Atlantic salmon under a wide variety of conditions. In my experience, hitching can be practiced on any salmon river in any water temperature. Fresh-run salmon usually respond to the method better than fish that have been in the river for a while, so it pays to try the hitch when the run is on.

I prefer to use a single-handed rod when I'm hitching as I find it easier to strip line in order to control the speed of the fly. I use a two-handed rod, though, if there are lots of rocks sticking out of the water or if the river has a high current speed and I need to hold as much line as possible out of the water.

Cast down and across the river at a 45-dgree angle to the current. The fly should maintain a nice, even speed as it comes across the surface of the river. Sometimes, the fly needs some help in order to wake effectively, so you may need to actively strip the line in slower currents; in a faster push of water, you may have to change your angle or drop your tip as the fly comes across. When the fly draws a beautiful and even V as it comes across, you will know that it is hitching well.

Hitching with tube flies

It is not the hitched fly itself but rather the effect created by a hitched fly that a salmon finds so irresistible. Imagine Lee Wulff's surprise when the salmon hit the knot in his leader: it was not the knot that attracted the salmon but rather the subtle V-shaped wake that it made on the surface. Getting a single hook to hitch correctly can be tough; luckily, there are other options.

Hitch fishing had a serious renaissance when a couple of fly fishermen in Iceland started using plastic tube flies for hitching. They drilled a small hole just below the head of the

In general, a large salmon fly should move faster than the current, and a small fly should move slower than the current. By contrast, the hitched fly should move with the approximate speed of the current. When the hitched fly is fishing properly, the hook and the rear of the tube fly will be below water while the front end rides above the water.

fly and ran the leader through it and out the end of the tube; in doing so, the tube fly skated perfectly across the current instead of diving beneath it. Plastic tubes flies are easier to wake than flies tied on single hooks; they also allow the angler to change both the size and the type of hook to suit the situation.

Tube flies for hitching are far from complicated. I use small, lightly dressed plastic tubes from ⅕ to ⅗ inches in length. I make a small hole in the tube with a darning needle approximately one-fifth of the way down the tube from the head of the fly. I warm the point of the needle with a lighter (make sure you hold the needle with a pair of pliers) before making the hole; warming the needle melts the plastic and leaves a perfect hole.

Where you make the hole in the tube fly is absolutely vital. The hole is made on the underside of the tube directly opposite the wing of the tube fly. For that reason, I usually tie tube flies that I will use for hitching without a throat hackle. I don't want anything to get in the way of the leader where it runs through the tube. It makes sense to head out to the river to make sure the fly is hitching correctly. If the fly refuses to hitch properly, you will have to make a new hole above or below the old one.

As plastic tube flies are short and sparsely dressed, it is important to use the right hooks. Trebles in sizes 12 to 18 are suitable; anything larger will usually drown the fly. Small hooks provide a very secure grip in the mouth of a fish; in

fact, I seldom use flies that are tied on anything larger than a size 8 hook, except when I am fishing large rivers with heavy currents, where large sunray shadows can be effective. In that case, I use a clove knot to get the fly to hitch. Put the knot underneath the wing or on the side of a single hook. If you are fishing the left bank going downstream, put the knot on the left side of the hook with the eye turned toward you.

A racket on the surface

There is no doubt that salmon (and sea trout) like flies that wake or create a racket on the surface. Long before the hitched fly was an accepted technique, the British writer Hugh Falkus described Yellow Dollies and Muddler Dollies in his superb books on salmon and sea trout fishing. Both of these patterns continue to produce well when greased or hitched in order to make them wake on top.

It is critical to change the size of a hitched tube fly in order to make a larger or smaller trailing V-shaped wake. The effect must be neither too vigorous nor too weak. In the case of the former, the fish is frightened; if the trailing V is too weak, the fly does not attract the fish. A hitched fly should move with the speed of the current. The hook and tube are below the water and the front rides above the water.

Foam flies

A lot has been written about foam flies for Atlantic salmon, and they certainly work. In my experience, however, foam

Nothing is more exciting than seeing a big salmon breaking the surface and taking the hitch.

flies wake almost too well: bright fish, in particular, seem to prefer a hitched fly that wakes with a more subdued action.

Things are different if the fish have been in the river for while: they may need a fly that is waking more vigorously in order to entice them.

A short cast and a short leader

For a hitched fly to fish properly, the leader should be short—no more than 9 to 12 feet, depending on whether you are using a single- or double-handed rod. If the leader is much longer, the fly is more difficult to control and the current has a tendency to grab the fly and pull it under.

The casts should be short: no more than 30 to 50 feet measured from the rod handle to the fly. Cast at a 45-degree angle down and across the current; if you cast more directly across the current, the fly will usually sink and fail to hitch correctly.

The cast must straighten out every single time and should begin to wake the moment it hits the surface. Because the leader is short, it sometimes straightens out too fast and the fly lands with a splash. Make sure that you slow down your casting tempo and lower your rod hand after you stop the rod at the end of the forward cast in order to ensure a more delicate presentation.

When a trout or a salmon takes a dead-drift dry fly, it rises more or less vertically through the water column and takes the fly as it floats through his window. As a hitched fly wakes

Releasing a huge salmon that could not resist the micro hitch in the Bonaventure in Gaspe, Canada.

across the fish's field of view, the salmon is forced to chase and catch the fly. As he chases down his prey, he generates a big wave behind the fly and takes the hitched fly with a savage slash. It is this reaction to my fly that makes me reach for a hitched fly before any other in my fly box.

A pair of modern 1 1/2 hand switch rods are waiting for a serious beat. Tierra del Fuego, Argentina.

Fly tackle

A good casting technique combined with correctly balanced tackle leads to optimal possibilities for well-executed fly casting and satisfying fly fishing. For that reason, this chapter deals with how to correctly choose and balance the fly tackle. If you are new to the challenges of fly casting, a set of well-balanced tackle will help you learn and practice the correct techniques. For the seasoned caster, tackle balance is a way to achieve the casts you need to efficiently cover the water. The better you are at adapting your tackle to a given situation and your own physique, the better fly fisher you'll become.

When fly fishermen discuss tackle, the debate can become rather overheated because there are many notions of the perfect tackle combination. And the rod, reel, and line commercials from manufacturers make it even harder to decide. Some fly fishermen believe that choice of tackle depends on individual casting style. Aggressive casters may prefer a relatively stiff rod, while casters with a more steady casting rhythm may find that a softer rod suits them better.

I believe both positions are incorrect. Good and efficient fly tackle should meet certain criteria, regardless of casting style and circumstances. The reel, for example, should be heavy enough to counterbalance the weight of the rod; if the reel is too light, the rod will appear tip-heavy during casting. The length and weight of the fly line and leader also have to suit the rod.

Figure 2-1. For the fly tackle to work optimally, line and leader must be 100 percent adapted to the rod.

> **In short, the fly tackle consists of the following:**
> 1. *The fly rod with reel and backing*
> 2. *The line system, which could be a double taper, a weight forward fly line, or a running line with loose shooting heads*
> 3. *The leader, such as polyleader or monofilament leader and fly (or flies, if fishing is done with more than one fly on the leader)*

Technically, the best line is not always the one that gives you the prettiest or the easiest casts. If rod, line, and leader combined cannot present the fly to the fish the way it is intended, the look of your cast doesn't matter. This chapter will give you several suggestions on how to choose your equipment so that you can handle any given fishing situation in the best possible way—and still get the prettiest and easiest cast.

Fishing tackle may consist of the best and most expensive single parts, but if rod, reel, line, leader, and fly do not work as a unit, the quality of each individual part is unimportant. A first-grade rod is worthless without a well-chosen line, and a good line is worth even less without a functional leader. Because good fishing tackle can be expensive, you need to spend your money where it matters most. Line and leader must be top-notch quality, and if the line and leader suit the rod, you can start with a midrange rod and reel.

Overall choice of tackle

The more rods and lines you have, the more difficult it can be to choose tackle for any given fishing situation. For that reason, I systematically estimate a number of conditions before I choose my tackle for the day.

To start, I always to consider which type of fly I need for the water. When I know the size of fly going on the leader, I then have an idea of the line weight I need: a large and heavy fly takes a heavier line (which equals a higher AFTM rating). The following table is a list of different line weights and the matching normal size flies for trout and salmon fishing with single-handed and double-handed rods.

Single-Handed Rod

AFTM line weight normal size of fly

  5 *Size 12-8 single hook*
  6 *Size 10-8 single or double hook*
  7 *Size 8 single or double hook*
  8 *Size 8-6 single or double hook and also ¼-inch brass tube*
 10 *Size 6-4 double hooks and also ¼-inch brass tube*

Double-handed rod

AFTM line weight normal size of fly

  7 *Size 10-8 single or double hook*
  8 *Size 8-4 single or double hook and also ¼-inch brass tube*
  9 *Size 6-4 double hook and also ¼-inch brass tube*
 10 *Size 6-4 double hook and also ¼–½-inch brass tube*
 11 *Size 4 double hook and also ½–1-inch brass tube*

Surroundings determine rod length

When I know the size of fly and weight of line, I look at the area surrounding the water. Are there trees, a steep bank, or other things that make overhand casting difficult? In that case, I'd choose a slightly longer rod than normal. A long rod will give a slower lift of the line, making it easier to do a Spey cast that will place the leader correctly on the water beside you and create a D-loop behind you. A longer rod also makes it easier to lift the line clear of rushes along the water's edge.

If waterside growth is not the main concern, use a slightly shorter rod, which is often easier to handle. You may be able to cover the water efficiently with a single-handed rod, but the double-handed rod is the obvious choice because the speed of the current varies across the stream. It will allow you to steer the fly during its course across the stream, mending and "parking" the fly in promising small lanes in the current. With this precise control, you can make the fly swing toward you or even away from you.

After sizing up all these conditions, you should have a clearer picture of which rod (single- or double-handed), rod length, and line weight you'll need to efficiently cover the water. Remember this simple rule of thumb: choose a rod based on the size of the stream, its surroundings, and line weight. Do not pick a rod based on the size of the fish you dream of catching. Your main concern is getting the fly out and fishing it effectively. With a bit of experience, it is really not that important whether you fight a big fish on a class 7/8 or 10/11 rod.

Choice of line and leader

After you have chosen the single- or double-handed rod that suits the water and the line weight best, it is time to decide on the type of line and leader. The deciding factor here is fly presentation. If the fly is going to fish high in the water or with short casts on a 6-weight single-handed rod or below, I prefer a floating weight-forward line with a long monofilament leader. This tackle gives an easy cast and a delicate presentation of the fly.

In stretches of water that need to be fished a little deeper, I prefer a line system where the casting part (the shooting head) and the leader can be easily changed if conditions dictate. My line of choice is a coated running line, a couple of loose bellies (shooting heads) in different densities, and an assortment of leaders (polyleaders) with different densities. All parts can be connected according to the loop-to-loop principle. (See figure 2-2.)

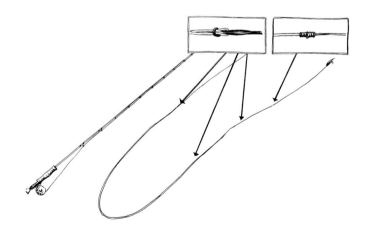

Figure 2-2. Loops are used to link the shooting head to the running line and leader. The leader is coupled to a middle piece of nylon monofilament, which is tied to the tip of the leader with a surgeon or blood knot.

A selection of three shooting heads and three leaders will provide opportunities to present the fly at different depths

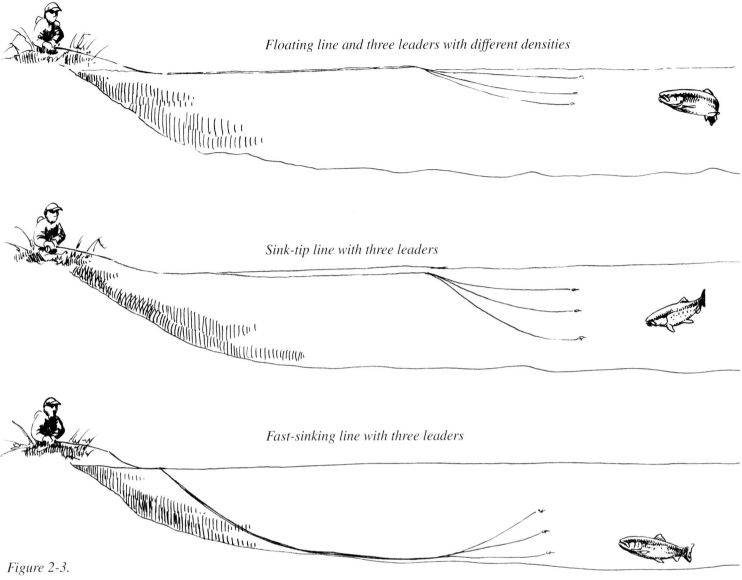

Floating line and three leaders with different densities

Sink-tip line with three leaders

Fast-sinking line with three leaders

Figure 2-3.

(see figure 2-3). The drawing shows the principle for the nine combinations of shooting heads and leaders.

- *Floating shooting head*
- *Floating shooting head with sink-tip*
- *Fast-sinking shooting head*

For each of these shooting heads you can choose among three different polyleaders: intermediate, sinking, and fast-sinking.

Bringing the fly down to the fish
Precisely how deep the fly will fish depends—apart from the mass of the line and leader—on the angle of the cast across the stream. The more you angle your line across the stream, the more pressure you'll see on the line and leader. More pressure lifts the fly up in the water, making it fish closer to the surface than it would have if the cast had been angled farther downstream.

How deep the fly is fishing also depends on how much slack you put in the line during the drift: a perfectly stretched cast will make the fly fish higher in the water.

In still water (lakes or coastal areas), how long you let fly, leader, and line sink before you start the retrieve determines the fishing depth. When coastal fishing for sea trout, for example, I usually choose a floating shooting head with an intermediate tip, a so-called sink-tip line.

I use an intermediate polyleader for leader that stretches well in the wind, since plenty of wind is a common factor on the coast. The sinking tip and the slow-sinking polyleader

A large sea-run brown is returned after a heavy fight on the River Irigoyen, Tierra del Fuego.

ensure that the fly sinks to a level where a hunting sea trout may spot it.

I also prefer a sink-tip line with an intermediate polyleader for salmon and sea trout fishing in larger rivers and streams.

If you supplement the sink-tip line with a fast-sink and superfast-sink polyleader, you have incredibly versatile and efficient equipment that is quite easy to cast.

Cast to the fish closest at hand

I commonly use polyleaders with different densities, except for surface fishing with a dry fly or riffling hitch, in which case I choose a floating line and a monofilament leader.

I do not use monofilament leaders for the rest of my fishing because the nylon's low density requires a long leader that is too long for close distance fishing. Polyleaders have a higher density, making it easier to present the fly delicately and precisely during short-distance fishing. In practical fishing, these leaders are highly effective.

I have a rule that I do not hesitate to call golden: It is far easier to catch the fish on your own side of the stream than the one across it.

During all these years of fishing, I have seen approximately as many fish on either side of the main current in an average river or stream! I bet you'll agree that you regularly see anglers who go through hell and back to catch the fish at the far side of the stream.

Running line and size of fly

Behind the shooting head is a coated running line. During casting, the running line maintains a lower speed than the upper line, so do not choose a running line that is too thin or too light to fulfill its mission in the cast. A thin running line also gives you less feeling of what is going on with the fly during the retrieve, especially if the temperature is down and your hands are numb with cold. (Read more about the function of the running line during casting on page 64.)

Fly rods with power

Fly rods have improved by leaps and bounds in recent years, a movement driven by skillful engineers in cooperation with knowledgeable rod designers. Today, you can purchase fly rods for under $100 that were the best money could buy only 10 to 15 years ago. Modern carbon technology has made rods light as feathers and exceedingly sturdy. These rods have actions that push the boundaries of what you can achieve with fly tackle. The result is that fly fishermen can cast and fish more efficiently than ever before.

The fly rod must fulfill certain basic demands. It has to be robust so that it can stand up to a certain degree of bruising yet light enough that you can fish a whole day without tiring. The rod building industry has actually become quite good at incorporating these two considerations into the blank, and even light carbon rods are far less fragile now than they were previously.

The blank should have a modern progressive action, making it easy to load the rod and allow presentation of the fly at all distances from 15 feet and out. Finally, the finished rod should include appropriate high quality fittings.

Following is a short description of how the rod should be built in order to make blank, eyes, ferrules (connections), reel seat, and rod handle work together as a unit.

The fly rod is fitted with a large stripping guide toward the handle and snake guides along the blank.

Guides on a fly rod

The guides on a fly rod are important because they affect the action of the blank while ensuring trouble-free casting and shooting of the line. The guides can either be fitted with one leg or two, the latter being more common. Many different types of guides have been manufactured over the years, but the two-legged snake guides seem to remain popular; they are light but relatively sturdy, work with all kinds of lines, and are inexpensive.

Rod action is affected by the weight of the guides and the wrappings attaching them to the rod. At the spots where the guides are attached, the rod is more rigid; however, the blank is made more flexible overall when it is mounted with guides. The number of guides on the blank is critical. Too few and the distance between the guides becomes too large and slack appears in the line, affecting the cast negatively.

Large guides result in less friction, making the line shoot better during casting. Overdimensioned guides are an advantage, but it is important that the guides suit the line weight: guides that are too large may result in slack line during casting and a loss of energy.

Apart from the snake guides, the rod should be fitted with two large stripping guides. On lighter single-handed rods, one is fine. The large guides give you trouble-free casting with a minimum of tangled running line, but during single- or double-haul casting, the stripping is greatly affected. To make the stripping guide more durable, it is often fitted with a ceramic ring.

On double-handed rods, commonly used in running water where any loose line will be carried downstream with the current, the lower stripping guides must be placed relatively far up the blank. A stripping guide placed far up the blank will reduce the angle on the loose line coming from downstream and carrying on through the guides in the cast. A stripping guide placed lower on the rod would result in a steeper angle and create a great deal of friction when the line has to be pulled off the water in the final cast forward.

A simple tip guide for trouble-free casting

Tip guides come in several types. Many manufacturers build their double-handed rods with a ceramic inlay tip guide. Unfortunately, a guide with ceramic inlay is often strength-

Use one of the guides on the rod as a fly rest.

ened behind the ring, creating a tendency for the connections on the line to snag on the part that strengthens the guide. It may also give you some unwanted trouble during the last phase of the fight, where the connection between leader and fly line often runs through the tip guide several times. In my experience, a hard metal guide with no inlay works best.

I now have all my rods fitted with a pear-shaped tip guide without supporting metal gadgets, and they haven't become worn for that reason. Even better, this kind of guide gives me longer and smoother casting on short and long distances alike, and at the same time, it works trouble-free during the fight.

Give the fly a rest—in a guide

Many fly rods are fitted with a small fly rest just above the handle, designed to hold the fly when it is not fishing. But the fly rest is basically redundant. When you move to a new stretch of water, for example, reel the line in until the loop connecting line and leader is just outside the tip guide. The leader is then led behind the reel along the blank, and the fly is secured in one of the guides along the top third of the rod.

This arrangement makes it simple to take out the fly and start fishing when you arrive at your next chosen spot. Otherwise, you would be forced to reel back the line, which is a struggle when the leader has to get back through the guides. Small time-saving details like these will pay off when you see a good fish rolling.

The ferrules of the fly rod

Today, most single-handed rods are made on three-piece blanks, while double-handed rods are often divided into four pieces. This gives the rods a sensible length for transport and eliminates the long rod-transport tube if the rod needs to be strapped to a backpack or stuffed in a duffel bag. The technology used to make ferrules has also improved, which means there is no noticeable difference between casting a three-piece rod compared to a two-piece or even a one-piece rod.

Keep in mind, however, that the ferrules are bound to be the weakest points on the rod, so I do not believe that the slightly shorter tube you get if your rod is in four or five parts justifies the extra ferrules. Actual travel rods are an exception: a five-piece rod is preferable to no rod at all, and I am pleased with a six-piece double-handed rod of $14\frac{1}{2}$ feet that often travels with me. But when you use that kind of rod, check the ferrules occasionally to make sure they are solidly locked down.

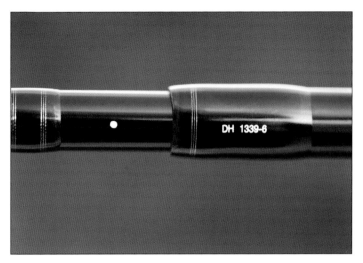

The fight butt keeps the reel out away from your body during fights.

A marking on the female and male ferrules will help you assemble the rod correctly.

The ferrules can be vulnerable, especially if the rod is not treated with care. Dirt and filth in the ferrule wears on the joint like coarse sandpaper, and after a while, the rod will work itself loose. Many rods are broken because the angler has neglected to check the ferrules for damage.

Many anglers choose to wrap the ferrules on double-handed rods in sticky tape to make sure that the ferrules do not loosen during fishing. I do not use this trick because I find that rod pieces usually work themselves loose when the rod is twisted during casting. It is a common mistake often connected with the position of the angler's feet, which makes the rod circle during casting. A better solution than using sticky tape is to rub the ferrules of the rod lightly with an ordinary candle. The wax will "cement" the parts more securely.

Reel seat

The reel seat has to be functional and hold the reel locked down, but that doesn't mean that it cannot be pretty to look at. For double-handed rods, I prefer a one-piece reel seat. On heavier single-handed rods, a reel seat extended with a fighting butt keeps the fly reel away from your body during fights. The fight butt supports the rod on your body, eliminating the risk of the reel getting tangled in your clothing and jamming. On a lighter rod, the fight butt may simply consist of a reel seat with an up lock that fastens the reel toward the handle.

Another practical quality of the fight butt is that it protects the reel by lifting it from the ground, so it is not easily damaged or bruised during a long day of fishing, in the many times you put the rod down to change the fly, loosen a knot on the leader, or enjoy a bite on land.

Fly reel

On a traditional fly reel, the diameter of the spool rapidly changes during a run. As the line leaves the spool, the diameter becomes smaller and the resistance of the drag becomes greater. When you have the fish on a long line, the pressure on the hook and leader increases, which means that the drag increases when you need it to decrease. Unfortunately, unless you are skilled enough to loosen the drag, there is a high probability that the fish will either break the leader or straighten the hook.

Instead, choose a large arbor reel. This type of reel gives you the best storage of the line because its large diameter allows you to wind in more line each time you turn the handle. Because the diameter doesn't change much, even if the line is peeled off dramatically during a run, the line does not become curly (as can happen with a traditional reel) and provides smoother brake during a fight.

A large arbor reel means larger windings and, as a result, a less curly line.

Modern carbon rods can be put through the most incredible tests—but they still have a problem with car doors closing on them. Miðfjarðará, Iceland.

It is self-evident that the reel seat should fit the reel that you intend to use on the rod. Previously, it was not unheard of to see reels with reel feet so "fat" that they couldn't fit some manufacturers' fly rods.

The fly reel can be too light

When you buy a fly reel, choose a sturdy model that can take some abuse. Of course, it also has to be able to take the amount of backing that you will need the day you see a "torpedo" tearing off downstream.

Keep in mind that the weight of the reel is important in relation to fly casting. On single-handed rods, the reel acts as a counterweight, and on heavier single-handed rods (8- and 9-weights and upward), a solid and slightly heavy reel will work well as a counterbalance. If you don't believe that the reel actually acts as a counterweight during the cast, try taking it off and casting with the rod alone; most people will cast poorly in such a situation. Without the reel as a counterweight, the rod will be tip-heavy and hard to load with energy.

Test to see if the tackle is balanced by placing a finger under the last cork ring in the handle (see the drawing below). If the reel end is a just a tiny bit heavier than the tip part, your tackle is in perfect balance.

On double-handed rods, the reel sits between your two hands as you cast, which means that weight is not the issue here. But again, a heavier reel will actually help you ease down the casting. When manufacturers of fishing tackle see it as their aim to produce the lightest tackle possible, I actually believe that it does more damage than good.

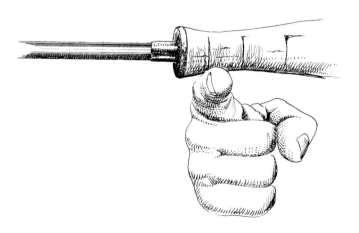

Do the finger test to check if the tackle is in balance.

A hand on the rim of the reel prevents an overrun when the fish is taking line from you.

Use the hand as a brake

The drag system of the reel is of no importance to the cast itself. The drag simply prevents line tangles when you strip line or when the fish takes line. I adjust the drag at a fairly light setting and prefer to adjust the drag during the fight by placing a hand on the protruding rim of the spool. By braking the fish this way, you can tell how much pressure to put on the fish, which will give you better control during the fight and a bigger catch.

As a fishing guide, I have seen many fish lost while the angler desperately tried to adjust the drag on the reel. In the heat of the fight, you can easily loosen the drag too much or tighten it altogether and stop the fish from running. In short, your hand is the best drag money can buy!

Heavy single-handed rod with a full Wells handle. The light single-handed rod below is fitted with a so-called half Wells handle.

The handles on single-handed rods

The handle is the connecting link between you and the rod. This is where the force from the casting movement is transmitted to the blank and then farther to the fly line. Despite its importance, the handle is a detail that many overlook.

The handle should be shaped in a way that makes it comfortable to hold, yet also in a way that helps you handle the rod correctly. The value of the handle for a sensible casting technique can hardly be overestimated, and a useless handle can spoil your chances of learning to cast properly.

The handle should be shaped in a way that allows you hold the rod firmly without unnecessary effort or unnaturally tightened muscles. If your grip on the rod is too loose, you won't be able to lead the rod back and forth in a controlled movement during the cast. The rod will wobble, resulting in a sloppy loop and a loss of control and energy.

The diameter of the handle is, to a certain degree, a matter of personal taste; but a thin handle may roll around in the palm of your hand, causing your grip on the rod to become forced and uncomfortable. It goes without saying that a handle like that won't help you cast well. If the handle is too thick, it will also be hard to hold in a relaxed way, and you will inevitably use too much force squeezing the rod handle.

Two types of cork handle

The picture above shows two traditional cork handles for single-handed rods. The upper handle is the full Wells type, which is mostly seen on powerful single-handed rods. The handle below is a so-called half Wells handle, mostly used on lighter single-handed rods up to 5/6 weight.

The half Wells handle is typically thinner than a full Wells handle and is used for close distance fishing where precision is a matter of importance. A thinner handle enables you to get a better feel for the soft tip action of a light rod.

The somewhat more powerful full Wells handle gives you a solid hold on the rod, making it easier to put some power into long casts.

The cork itself should be of the best possible quality, which will add years to the lifespan of the handle and feel better in the palm of your hand. During a long day of fishing, you'll find that having a handle made from first-grade cork is a big deal. Poor quality cork, which has many small grooves and holes, has to be covered with filler. Unfortunately, first-grade cork is hard to obtain, and even the best wineries now cork their bottles with plastic.

Figure 2-4. Wrong grip with the thumb on top of the rod.

Figure 2-4 shows a common, yet wrong way to hold the handle of the fly rod. When you grip the rod in this way, with the thumb on top of the rod, you will have a tendency to squeeze and push the rod forward, meaning only the tip section of the rod will be utilized. You will hear this quite clearly when the tip of the rod makes a swishing sound. Another fault with this grip is that your fingertips will touch the palm of your hand. This grip is uncomfortable and creates a loose grip because you cannot close your hand completely on the handle.

Instead, hold the handle as shown in figure 2-5 so your hand is evenly spread over a larger area of the handle. With this grip, the rod cannot twist and the movements of your arm are transmitted unhindered to the blank. This detail is important when your goal is to transmit energy from your arm to the fly rod. Notice that the thumb is not directly on top of or at the side of the handle; instead the thumb and index finger form a V shape.

Figure 2-5. Correct grip: The thumb and index finger form a V.

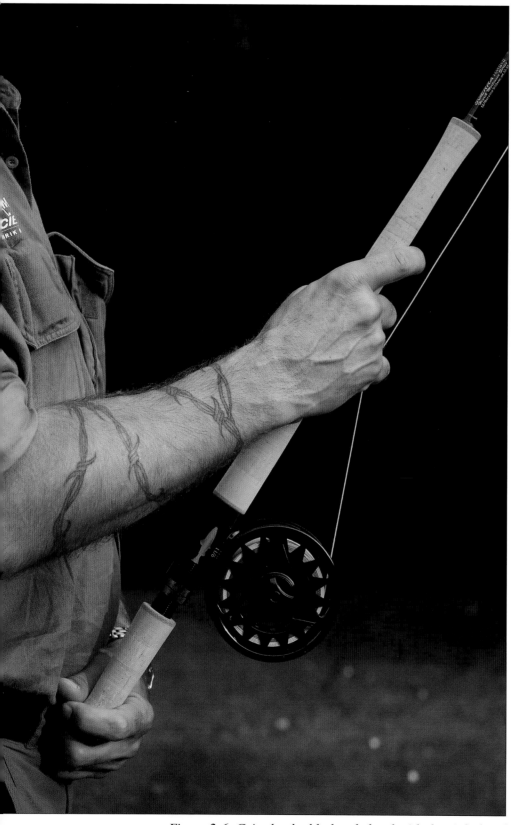

Figure 2-6. Grip the double-handed rod with the right hand on top. Both hands should form rings, and the right hand's grip must be quite loose.

The handle of the double-handed rod

One advantage of the double-handed rod is that you have both hands at your disposal, making it is less strenuous to keep a firm grip on the rod throughout a whole day's fishing. The two hands combined give you greater precision and more uniform casting.

The photo on page 38 shows a light 7/8-weight, double-handed rod on the left and a heavier 9/10-weight, double-handed rod on the right. The handles are identically shaped, but the handle on the lighter rod is a bit shorter because this rod is typically used for short, precise casting under tight conditions with smaller flies. The heavier rod is used for slightly longer casts, often with larger flies and sometimes with sinking lines. In those situations you need more force and larger movements of the rod, so a longer handle will give you more freedom of movement.

Gripping the double-handed rod

For the basic cast, hold the rod as shown in the photo on the left. Start by gripping the butt-cap with a ring-shaped grip, formed with your left hand thumb and index finger, and place your remaining three fingers for support. Then, adjust the grip of your right hand so that your lower arm is horizontal when your upper arm is straight down and the rod is in the front stop. If the horizontal and vertical positions are hard for you to match, simply find a comfortable casting position more or less like the one shown.

When you do short casts on 30–45 feet, move your right hand farther up the handle. This grip will give you greater precision in your casting because your right hand will control the cast. For longer casts, move the right hand toward the reel to achieve less lever movement. This change allows the rod to load deeper and increases the acceleration of the rod tip.

This is the starting position, but in double-handed casting, the trick is to be flexible and not lock yourself down to one particular position of your hands.

Use the starting position as a basis and try experimenting with the grip of the hand holding the top section of the handle until you find what grips work for you during different kinds of casts. In the real world—which for us means Mother Nature—you will need to cast from a range of positions, each demanding some ability to adapt.

The action of the rod

The concept of rod action is shrouded in mystery, but in fact, it just covers how a rod bends when it is loaded and subsequently straightens out. Rods have a distinct tip, medium or

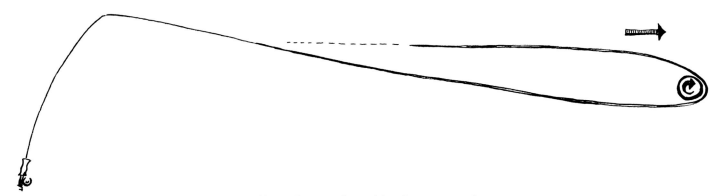

A rod with a progressive action gives a small "tip bounce," resulting in a narrow loop.

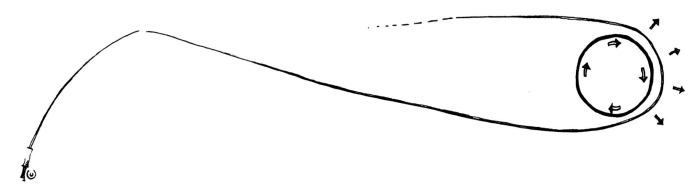

Figure 2-7. The full action rod bends too far forward, causing the loop to open.

full action. I prefer progressive rods, which means that the rods work the full length of the blank even at a moderate load without appearing floppy. The following part of this chapter explains why the progressive action is ideal and how this action, in combination with correct casting style, ensures that the whole blank is used.

As seen in chapter 1 when we dealt with the physics of fly casting, one of the basic rules states that the line will follow the movements of the tip guide; figure 2-7 shows how the movement of the tip guide depends on rod action. The top drawing shows a rod with a progressive action: the rod follows the movements of the caster and works even at moderate strain throughout its length, and then the rod settles down when the arm casting it is at rest. These factors combined—a result of the right casting movement—work to build the loop.

Full action—bends too much

In the bottom drawing in figure 2-7, a correct casting movement is still used, but the rod has an old-fashioned full action. It is loaded correctly, but when the cast is delivered, the rod bends too far forward before it straightens out. The forward bend of the rod in the front stop is so excessive that the loop

becomes too large. When the rod straightens back out, a series of wavelike movements, clearly visible to the caster, build up along the lower line. Under these circumstances, a full action rod takes longer to settle down. The poor dampening qualities of this rod will give you some noise on the line in the shape of an unsteady loop, which will lead to a loss of energy and poor presentation of the fly.

The difference between a soft full action rod and a rod with progressive action is tangible. The progressive action rod is not the same as a stiff rod. It, too, bends deeply when loaded, but without the excessive movements of the tip.

Tip action—a stiff stick!

A stiff rod, which is called a tip action rod or a fast rod by many manufacturers, is probably the hardest rod to cast with because you lose the feel of the dynamics of the cast, the blank, and the line. Rods with tip action also have problems with short-distance presentation. To compensate, they cast a long way if you work hard with them; in my opinion, this benefit is only relevant in the sport of casting, where length is everything. Distance casting, on the other hand, has little in common with practical fly fishing. The question is whether fighting a fish on such a stiff stick may be less fun.

Rod, line, and leader have done their job, now it's up to the fly and the angler to do the rest. Árbæjarfoss, West Rangá, Iceland.

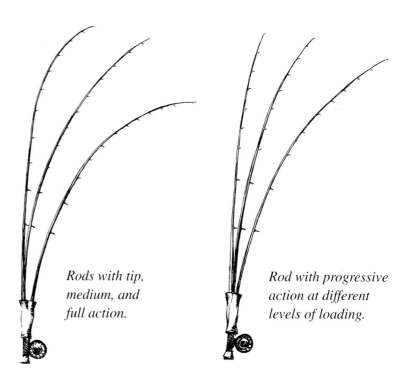

Rods with tip, medium, and full action.

Rod with progressive action at different levels of loading.

Figure 2-8.

Progressive action—works from tip to butt

The optimal progressive fly blank is built to work through its entire length, even at moderate strain. At higher strain, the blank bends deeper through its entire length. At the same time it is important that the rod settles down fast after forceful exertion, a quality referred to as good dampening properties. Figure 2-8, left, shows the three classic actions: tip action, medium action, and full action. In comparison, figure 2-8, right, shows a modern progressive action at three different levels of loading.

Conversely, a full action rod bends at moderate strain yet still takes a while to settle down. When you cast a long line on a full action rod, the rod will have a larger field of movement because it bends deeply in both directions during both loading and off-loading. The result is poor precision in the cast.

The effect of the progressive action is that the whole blank flexes at all rates of loading, and when the load increases, it works deeper throughout its entire length.

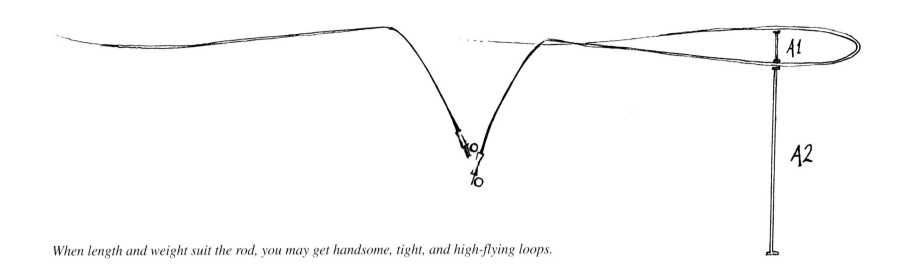

When length and weight suit the rod, you may get handsome, tight, and high-flying loops.

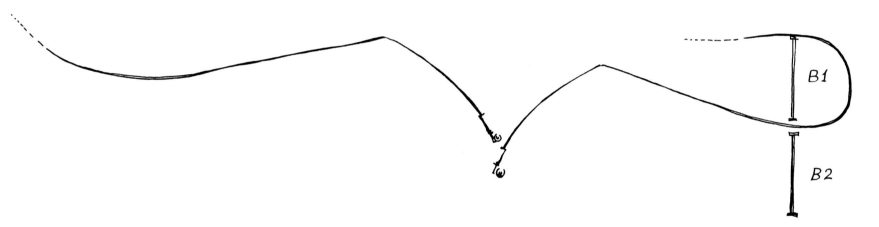

Figure 2-9. If the line is too heavy, the rod is overloaded—the loops become open and hard to handle.

At the same time, the blank contains superb dampening qualities, ensuring optimal control in the final phase of the cast. The progressive action is truly a modern full action.

Whichever rod you use, the action of the rod will always be connected to the line being cast.

Figure 2-9, top, shows how a line of suitable length and weight would hang in the air during the ideal forward cast.

In the lower drawing, the angler is using a line that is much too heavy. This situation happens when eager beginners make shooting heads out of a double-taper line, which is cut in half and then whittled down farther until they feel that the belly suits the rod.

Too much focus is placed on weight, however, as opposed to length, when the goal is a longer cast.

The problem is that the rod is forced to work differently than intended by the rod designer.

Chapter 3

Backing, Running Line, Bellies and Leaders

The line system consists of the running line, an assortment of bellies, and leaders with different sinking rates.

Money out the window

Far too often I see anglers spending huge sums on fancy rods, convinced that money can buy them great casting. And yet their tackle and line end up being close to worthless because all their money went into the rod. Rod advertisements are designed to make you believe that expensive rods can cast to the moon all by themselves, which of course they can't. And with a poor substitute for a proper line, they can't even cast as far as your garden gate.

In short, the rod is not the most important piece of fly-fishing equipment. A good line system—with a running line, belly, and leader—is.

Let's assume that you have purchased "the best rod in the world," but you only have a second-rate line at your disposal. In such a situation, you won't ever be able to utilize the full potential of that fabulous rod. Furthermore, your control in the cast and when you present the fly will be less than perfect. If, on the other hand, you bought a run-of-the-mill rod, but a perfectly adapted line system, then you would be able to cast and fish more than adequately. In order to utilize a rod fully, you need a perfectly adapted combination of running line, belly, and leader.

This chapter is dedicated to choosing and composing the gear that really does make a difference: the individual parts of the line system.

The backing

Closest to the spool axis is an amount of backing, a reserve for the day when the really big fish decides to swim toward blue water or down the river with the entire fly line and running line behind it. In truth, this scenario is most likely to happen only in an angler's dreams. Throughout the years, I have landed thousands of trout and salmon; I have seen my backing racing through the tip guide once or twice.

In fact, if you've got the entire fly line plus 50 yards or more of backing outside the tip guide, the pressure on the leader will break it easily unless you have lots of experience fighting big fish and you can keep your cool. Such a critical moment is not the time to test a rod to its limit.

The backing serves two purposes. The first one, as described above, is insurance if a big fish decides to swim downstream to a pool that you cannot reach from the bank. The second is to make the diameter of the axis as big as possible. The fly line becomes less prone to curl and you can retrieve slack line faster when the spool's diameter is bigger.

Err on the side of caution and supply your reel with at least 100 yards of backing to make the spool diameter as wide as possible; more backing on the reel is a plus. Remember, however, that the reel also has to contain your fly line and leader.

I always use woven Dacron as backing. (The breaking strain of the backing is in English pounds. A pound is about 445 grams.) For trout fishing, choose a backing of at least 15 to 20 pounds. The backing for salmon fishing should be 30 to 40 pounds.

The line system

The fly line is a vital part of the equipment, and the most important qualities of a line are tapering and density.

The word "tapering" denotes the profile of the line, or the diameter on any given spot along the length of the line. It tells you how the mass of the line is distributed along its length. Tapering is important in relation to the cast ability of the line, or how the line loads the rod and how it moves through the air.

The specific gravity is the weight of the line per square unit; typically this measuring unit is grams per cubic centimeter. Basically, the specific gravity determines whether the line floats or sinks, and in the latter case, if it sinks fast or slowly. In fishing terms, specific gravity is responsible for where the fly is presented to the fish: near the surface or close to the bottom.

The actual weight of the line is important when you have to match line and rod. The line weight is rarely stated explicitly on the package. It is decided from the tapering and density, but this implies that you know both, and that you know how to calculate the answer. Instead, look for the AFTM classification, which groups lines in classes from 0 to 15. (For more on the AFTM system, see The weight of the fly line on page 57.)

> ### Line coding
> Few line manufacturers supply detailed information about line profiles or specific gravity. Instead, the normal procedure is to label the line with a code consisting of three parts. A line labeled "WF-7-F" tells us that the line is weight-forward tapering (WF), AFTM class 7, and floating (F). The code gives you all the important information you need.

A landscape where the wind can really pick up speed. If the casting style is adapted to it, though, the wind can be your friend. Rio Grande, Argentina.

Abbreviations for fly lines

F	=	*floating*
S	=	*sinking*
I	=	*intermediate (the line has approximately the same mass as water and typically hovers just below the surface)*
WF	=	*weight forward*
DT	=	*double taper*
ST	=	*shooting taper (a relatively short belly, 8–12 meters [24–36 feet] and usually a bit heavy)*
LB	=	*long belly (extra long belly)*

Taperings

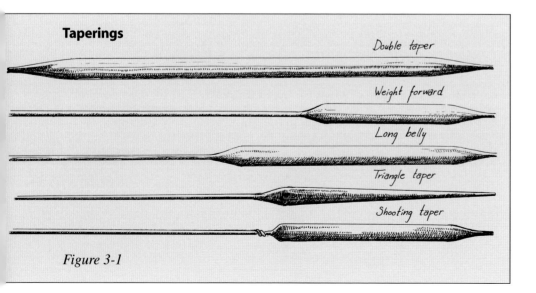

Figure 3-1

The tapering of the fly line

The huge choice of fly lines today can be confusing. Basically all lines are double-taper or weight-forward lines. The weight on the latter type of line is also called the belly because it sits on the line like a belly.

Figure 3-1 shows the most common taperings for fly lines. At the top, a double taper (DT) consists of a thick middle section that tapers toward each end. Double-taper lines are not widely used today, but they still have sworn followers who would never dream of using anything else for dry-fly fishing or salmon fishing with double-handed rods.

Below the DT, three different weight-forward (WF) lines are shown. The weight-forward line consists of a thick casting belly at the front and a thinner running line behind. The belly is tapered toward the tip (front taper), just like the double taper. Toward the running line, the belly has a similar tapering (back taper). Weight-forward lines are the dominant line type today, and a wide selection is available.

The bottom line is a shooting taper (ST) attached to a loose running line. Notice that the only difference between the shooting head and the weight forward is the fact that the belly and running line are connected by a loop. Because they are similar, they cast more or less in the same way.

The most important difference among the versions is the length of the belly, and the figure shows three different types: short belly, long belly, and the Lee Wulff Triangle Taper.

Many anglers associate the shooting head with a too-heavy belly and a thin running line, but such a combination is definitely unsuitable for practical fishing. Heavy artillery like this can cast a long way, if it is coupled with a stiff rod, but line control is blown to the wind—and what is the point of casting a long way if it all lands in a pile in the horizon?

The bellies of modern shooting heads are designed much like weight-forward bellies and are often referred to as "modified weight-forward lines," which is a precise description of the shooting head systems I use. In my opinion, the weight-forward line is, without doubt, the best line ever made for fly fishing. My aim has been to keep all the good qualities and the fine presentation connected with the weight-forward line, while making it easy to adapt the tackle to every fishing situation. The result is a flexible system in which the individual parts are connected with loops, which makes it easy to change the profile and mass/weight of the line.

If, for example, you fish in the top layer of the water and arrive at a stretch of water demanding a deeper approach, all you have to do is to replace the floating line with a sinking belly—a switch that doesn't take longer than changing a lure on a spinning rod. The fly fisher is suddenly able to adapt and change lines according to conditions with a minimum of hassle. Another great advantage is that this system is adapted, which means that no matter which combination you choose, the casting weight stays constant—the rod is loaded with the same casting weight if you choose a floating, sink tip, or fast sinking line.

The front taper of the line is important in relation to the kind of leader you choose, whether it's DT or WF lines or a shooting head. As a line designer, I often choose to give the belly a relatively short front taper. This makes the lines work well with relatively long leaders. If line and leader stretch softly and harmoniously in the forward cast, it is because the line is loaded with energy. This energy is gradually sapped from the tip part of the fly line and the leader, both of which are tapered. If the tip of the fly line and leader weren't tapered, the wheel in the loop would roll out with too much power, making the fly land with a clumsy splash. The softening effect at the end of the cast is due to the fact that the line is thinner. By using a shorter front taper, you can tie on a much longer leader, which will still stretch properly.

Suitably long leaders give you an advantage during practical fishing. The distance from the fly line to the fly is increased, which means that the risk of the fish being scared by the fly line is reduced.

The long leader is a necessity if you wish to do the Scandinavian Spey cast. If the leader is too short, the surface tension holding the leader down during the cast is reduced, which means that the leader loses its grip on the surface and the cast collapses. The opposite scenario is the case with some English and especially American line designs with very long front tapers. As a rule, these kinds of lines are useless with long leaders, and they force you to use the leader as well as the front taper as an anchor when you want to do a Spey cast. The inevitable result is that you disturb the water more, which means more spooked fish and poorer fly fishing.

The weight of the fly line

A fly line should have a specific weight in order to work with your rod of choice. Since the early 1960s, the weight of fly lines has been classified by the AFTM scale, which goes from 1 to 15. AFTM is short for American Fishing Tackle Manufacturers' association; hence the scale was called AFTMA. The classes 0 and 13 to 15 were not on the original list but were added later.

Exactly which class a line belongs to is determined by weighing the top front 9.14 meters (30 feet). This means that a line in AFTM class 7 should weigh between 11.5 and 12.5 grams on the front 9.14 meters; this is the same regardless of tapering and specific gravity of the line. A line of class 7 thus weighs the same whether it's a floating DT or fast sinking WF.

Fly Line Weights

The weights in this table are given in grains and grams, along with the allowed deviation.

Line class	Weight (grains)	Weight (grams)
0	56 ± 2	3.6 ± 0.1
1	60 ± 6	3.9 ± 0.4
2	80 ± 6	5.2 ± 0.4
3	100 ± 6	6.5 ± 0.4
4	120 ± 6	7.8 ± 0.4
5	140 ± 6	9.1 ± 0.4
6	160 ± 8	10.4 ± 0.5
7	185 ± 8	12.0 ± 0.5
8	210 ± 8	13.6 ± 0.5
9	240 ± 10	15.6 ± 0.6
10	280 ± 10	18.1 ± 0.6
11	330 ± 12	21.4 ± 0.8
12	380 ± 12	24.6 ± 0.8
13	450 ± 15	29.2 ± 1.0
14	500 ± 15	32.4 ± 1.0
15	550 ± 15	35.6 ± 1.0

Fly line weight was originally calculated by the American measuring unit grains, which is the same as 64.8 mg (0.0648 g). Now that we are on the topic of units, remember that a foot is the same as 30.48 cm, and that a foot is divided into 12 inches, each measuring 2.54 cm. A foot is written 1' and an inch 1". This means that a fly rod of 9' 6" is 9 foot 6 inches long or just less than 290 centimeters.

Measures and weights		
1 grain	*=*	*64.8 milligrams (0.0648 gram)*
1 pound (lb)	*=*	*454 grams*
1 inch	*=*	*2.54 centimeters*
1 foot	*=*	*30.48 centimeters*

The limitations of the AFTM system

Two recommended line classes are often written on fly rods: for example, # 8/9. This means that the rod works best with a class 8 double-taper line or a class 9 weight-forward line. If you choose to fish with loose bellies (shooting heads), choose a class 9 line for the rod in question.

The AFTM system was developed with single-handed rods and corresponding lines in mind. If you're fishing with double-handed rods, the system misses the target entirely. Despite the qualities of the AFTM system, you cannot use a single-handed line of one class for a double-handed rod of the same class. A line for a single-handed rod, AFTM class 9, suits a single-handed rod class 9. The same line would be far too light for a double-handed rod classified the same way. Check the package before you buy a line, making sure it clearly states that the line is for a double-handed rod. Be equally attentive when you buy lines for single-handed rods.

Another weakness of the AFTM system is that it only refers to the last 30 feet of the line without any thought for the remaining part of the line.

A typical weight-forward line is made with a belly that is longer than 9.14 meters, so it weighs more than the weight stated in the AFTM scale. When you do longer casts, the belly will typically hang just outside the tip guide, which means that the rod is loaded with a weight that is considerably higher than the line weight for the last 9.14 meters. This is why a rod classified as an 8/9 weight works well with a standard weight-forward line class 9, while with a long belly line of the same class, it is loaded too much. The weight of a long belly line class 8 is more like the weight of a standard class 9 weight-forward line. The AFTM system pays no heed to this fact.

An alternative to the AFTM system

Presently, new ways of classifying fly lines are appearing. I doubt that they will make life easier for the fly fisher; it is likely that they will add to the confusion.

You could ask yourself why the classification system for spinning rods is more or less ignored. On a spinning rod you can see the recommended casting weight, for example, 10–15 grams, which tells the angler that the rod performs best with lures weighing 10–15 grams. Nothing would be simpler than for fly rod manufacturers to state the recommended weight of belly for the rod in question.

Fortunately, several line manufacturers have already addressed that challenge and label their lines by AFTM class, the weight of the belly in grams, and the length in meters, making it far easier to match different line types for the same rod. Once you know which weight suits the rod (in grams), the rest is merely a matter of choosing the line with the corresponding belly-weight.

Figure 3-2. Two fly rods in the same line class have markedly different casting weights. The single-handed rod on top takes a casting belly of 17.5 grams, while the double-handed rod below casts optimally with a belly of 19–21 grams. This example clearly shows the weakness of the AFTM system.

Rods labeled with the casting weight (in grams) that the rod's designer finds suitable are a big step in the right direction. Figure 3-2, top, shows a single-handed rod of 9 feet, 6 inches (290 centimeters), which casts optimally with either a double-taper line class 7 or a weight-forward line (or loose belly) class 9. It also shows that the rod works the best with a casting weight of 17.5 grams.

Figure 3-3. Look for lines that are labeled with length, weight, and line class. The line shown above is a sink-tip shooting head class 8 for single-handed rods. It measures 9.8 meters and weighs 17.5 grams.

Shooting heads for single-handed rods

Today, shooting heads are labeled with AFTM class as well as the length and weight of the belly. The table on this page lists weight (grains) and length (feet and inches) of three different varieties of fly lines: floating line (F), Floating line with sinking tip (F/I), and sinking line (S).

The lines suit single-handed rods in AFTM classes 5/6, 6/7, 7/8, and 8/9. The system is developed to make fly casting and tackle composition as simple as possible. This means that even though the lengths of the different bellies vary, the bellies within the same class weigh the same. In other words, the rod is loaded and casts the same way whether the belly is floating, sink tip, or fast sinking. In my own experience,

I have found that the combinations of length and weight for these casting bellies work well.

Line class	F	F/I	Sink rate 6
5	*170 grains / 33'6"*	*170 grains / 32'10"*	*170 grains / 23'*
6	*216 grains / 34'9"*	*216 grains / 33'6"*	*216 grains / 26'3"*
7	*239 grains / 35'1"*	*239 grains / 33'10"*	*239 grains / 26'3"*
8	*262 grains / 35'1"*	*262 grains / 33'10"*	*262 grains / 29'6"*

Shooting heads for single-handed rods

Your first impression of a sink 6 line may be that it seems overly heavy, but often it is the right choice when you wish to fish the fly close to the bottom. A sink 6 line descends 6 inches (15 centimeters) per second. If the line is complemented with polyleaders in three different densities, it is possible to fish the fly really close to the bottom without getting stuck. Known as a "killer's approach," this method works for not only trout and grayling, but also when your quarry is salmon, sea trout, or steelhead.

You may find it hard to raise a salmon or a sea trout to the surface at times. These fish spend most of their time near the bottom where the current is weakest. Most fishermen use a sinking line for early season fishing in cold spring rivers for first fresh-run salmon and sea trout (first springers, May springers, etc.). But the sinking line comes into its own for late season fishing when grumpy old salmon and sea trout need to see a fly right in front of their noses before they show any interest at all. Even in the middle of the summer, when the water runs low in the stream, I choose a sinking line to reach salmon and sea trout that rest in the deepest holes.

Line class

To underline how inappropriate the AFTM scale is for classification of double-handed lines, compare the shooting heads for single-handed rods in class 7/8 and 8/9 on this page to the ones on the next page. The difference between the lines in class 7/8 for single-handed rods and those for double-handed rods is 4.5 grams; for class 8/9, it is a significant 9 grams. Notice that the table does not show the heaviest lines available on the market for the classes in question, so the significant differences between the lines are not extreme. This analysis points to the obvious: double-handed lines should have their own AFTM standard (see also figure 3-2).

Line class	F	F/I	Sink rate 2	Sink rate 3/4	Sink rate 4/5	Sink rate 6
7/8	309 grains / 32'10"	309 grains / 32'2"	309 grains / 29'2"	309 grains / 29'2"	309 grains / 29'2"	309 grains / 26'3"
8/9	401 grains / 34'1"	401 grains / 33'2"	401 grains / 32'2"	401 grains / 32'2"	401 grains / 32'2"	401 grains / 29'10"
9/10	509 grains / 37'5"	509 grains / 36'5"	509 grains / 34'9"	509 grains / 34'9"	509 grains / 34'9"	509 grains / 32'10"
10/11	556 grains / 39'8"	556 grains / 38'5"	540 grains / 36'1"	540 grains / 36'1"	540 grains / 36'1"	540 grains / 34'9"

Shooting heads for double-handed rods.

Shooting heads for double-handed rods

Double-handed rods are usually used for bigger and often deeper streams with heavy currents. You will find the wider assortment of sinking lines with different densities useful.

If you combine the selection of sinking lines with a floating line and a sink tip line (F/I), you will be able to present the fly from the surface down to the bottom.

The same principle applies for the double-handed lines; the weights for the various line lengths are constant within a line class in the shooting-head system.

Sink 3/4 and 4/5 are lines with two sink rates. On the sink 3/4 line, the tip of the belly is sink 4 while the remaining part is sink 3. The advantage with such a design is that the thin part of the line sinks with the same rate as the thicker part of the belly. If the specific gravity were constant throughout the line, the thicker part would descend faster than the thinner part. To even out the disparity, the specific gravity of the thinner part is higher. These equalized lines are suitable for fishing in rivers and streams with a fairly even current where the pressure on the line is the same no matter where it is under the surface.

Two regular sinking lines are also included in the table: sink 2 and sink 6. These lines descend with the same speed. These types of lines are suitable for large rivers that move large quantities of water at many different speeds from top to bottom. In this kind of water, sinking lines like the two described will settle more or less in the same layer of water and fish that layer of the water at the same speed. The sink 2 line is designed for fishing in the top part of the water current; the sink 6 line penetrates the hard currents, making the fly fish near the bottom.

The current in a river is stronger and faster from the middle of the water column to the surface, while it moves slower toward the bottom. Imagine casting a sink 2/6 (sink 2 in the thicker rear part of the line and sink 6 in the thin tip section) across the river: the tip will descend toward the bottom while the rear end will ride closer to the surface. The rear end of the line is affected by the strong current, which will constantly pull the line and fly up toward the surface. This scenario means that the fly will never fish close to the bottom, despite the fact that the tip half of the line has the higher sinking rate.

Heavyweight arguments for sinking lines

Floating lines have been widely used for many years, but sinking lines are gaining popularity for at least two reasons. First, they cast well. The high specific gravity gives sinking lines a small diameter, and thinner lines generate less wind resistance. This is why sinking lines cut through a tricky wind better than a floating line. Second, sinking lines are better for an approach where the fly is fished deep.

Even in a small stream, a floating line with a fast sinking polyleader is not enough to make the fly fish near the bottom. Contact with the fly is often very poor because a sharp angle appears on the line between the floating line on the surface and the leader cutting through the water (see the illustrations on page 39). A good sinking line, however, will sink its entire length, bringing the fly level with the fish yet ensuring that you are in complete contact with the fly throughout your swing.

Sinking lines are used less because most fishermen find a sinking line hard to handle when it is lifted from the water. But with the right technique, lifting a sinking line is as easy as lifting a floating line (turn to chapter 8, Casting with a sinking line, for more information). Traditional sinking lines, which sink uniformly in their entire length, are the right choice when your task is to get through a roaring current in spate.

In other situations, however, you'll find more advantages in fishing and casting using a line that sinks faster toward the tip. Such a line gives you a visual indication of how the fly is fishing, because the part closest to you sinks slower and therefore remains in sight. This line is easier to lift clear of the water because the line indicates where it is by the angle it descends through the water, giving you a clue as to how to raise it.

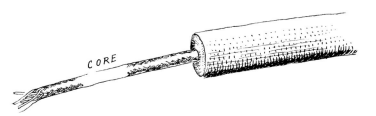

Floating line with Dacron core.

Figure 3-4. Sinking line with Dacron core.

The core of the fly line

The core is the foundation of the fly line and gives it a very high breaking point. It is surrounded by plastic material that gives the fly line its floating or sinking properties, including its sinking speed.

The most common way to make a fly line, by far, is shown in figure 3-4. A core of woven Dacron is embedded in the center of the fly line. The drawing shows a cross section of two fly lines with the same weight per measuring unit. The cores of the lines are identical, which means that the different properties of the fly lines are determined by the coating. The line on top is a floating line, while the bottom one is a sinking line.

The standard material for manufacturers of fly line cores has, for many years, been woven Dacron. You can also find lines with cores made from monofilament nylon or woven nylon. In most cases, these are specialized lines for tropical saltwater fly fishing, where a stiffer fly line is required. In hot water and baking sun, the stiff fly line becomes supple enough for fine fly fishing for speedy swimmers like bonefish and tarpon.

But don't try the same tropical fly line for fishing in northern climates. In the cold saltwater, like you'll find fishing for sea trout on the Scandinavia shore, a tropical fly line will become as stiff as uncooked spaghetti. Conversely, if you take a cold-water line with Dacron core fishing in tropical climes, it will act like spaghetti cooked *al dente*.

Low stretch lines

Dacron is a tried and tested material with many fine merits, but it also has a couple of disadvantages. One is that the lines are elastic and have a memory, making them adopt the shape of the spool they are stored on. For this reason, Dacron lines have to be stretched before they are used; otherwise, they won't work properly.

Newer lines have been developed with a low-stretch core of woven Kevlar, which is almost completely nonstretch. Don't confuse these lines with the first generation of Kevlar lines, which reached the shops in the early 1990s; they were useless because they snapped in two without warning. The big advantage of the new lines with low-stretch cores is that you don't have to stretch them before you start casting; they are born without a memory. They cast flies smoothly, and the nonstretch quality gives you excellent feel when you fish the fly. The improved contact is especially significant in the magic moment when a fish decides to hit the fly. Best of all, you can still make your own loops on the fly line because the low stretch core is made in the same way as a Dacron core.

The coating of the fly line

In fly line manufacturing, the choice of coating is quite complicated. Apart from specific gravity, the coating also affects how the line behaves in differing water temperatures. A line that performs well during midsummer fishing in the stream or salmon river where water temperatures reach 68° F can become stiff and hard to handle when water temperatures drop below 41° F. Conversely, lines that work well during cold conditions become soft and almost sticky when temperatures are high. So keep in mind that cold- and warm-water lines are not just a trick of the trade.

Another factor of line coating is the durability of the line. In my experience, really slick fly lines often have a soft surface and wear faster. These slick fly lines also slow down considerably when they touch the blank during casting. The more granular-feeling lines, however, seem to bounce off the blank, which leads me to prefer lines with a slightly coarse surface; they are more durable and they are slowed down less on contact with the blank. Unfortunately, a line with a coarse surface also makes more noise in the guides. But this disadvantage is minor when compared with the advantages.

One last thing about lines: all fly lines, regardless of make, need a helping hand once in a while. The solution is to use a line conditioner (read more about tackle maintenance in chapter 9).

The running line is free to whiz through the guides toward the horizon. Coastal fishing on Langeland, Denmark.

Adaptation of loose bellies

If you wish to adapt loose bellies (shooting heads) for your fly rod of choice, make sure the length and the weight are suitable for the kinds of casts you want to perform. (Check the same things when you have to choose a whole WF line.) Please note that the deviations from the optimal weight or length differ for overhead and Spey casting.

As a point of reference, consider a hypothetical experiment with a single-handed rod of $9\frac{1}{2}$ feet with an optimal casting weight of 14 grams. This rod would typically be classified as a 6/7 in the AFTM scale. In order to cover a range of fishing situations, you'll need a line that can overhead cast as well as Spey cast. This is where my experience tells me that a really good all-around length for both types of casts on varying distances is a belly of 10.5 meters.

One day, however, you may find that the good 10.5 meter, 14 grams belly has been left behind in your tackle room. Instead, you dig out four loose bellies like the ones shown in figure 3-5. They are all floating and with weights and lengths described below. Which do you choose?

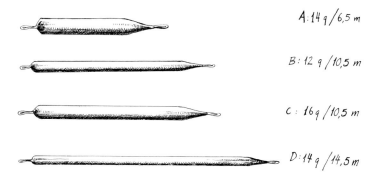

Figure 3-5.

Belly	Weight	Length
A	216 grains	21'4"
B	185 grains	34'5"
C	247 grains	34'5"
D	216 grains	47'7"

Compared to the ideal casting belly of 10.5 meters and 14 grams, all four bellies represent a potential limitations. Lines A and D weigh the same as the ideal weight for the rod, but one is too short and the other is rather long. The lengths of line B and C, on the other hand, are suitable but the first is too light and the other is slightly too heavy.

In overhead casting, the weight of the belly is critical: you don't have to think about forming a dynamic D-loop behind you like you do in a Spey cast. The more pressing issue is to use a line with the exact weight to optimally load the rod. For all-around use, a length of 10.5 meters is fine, but you can overhead cast with longer or shorter bellies.

The short belly, A, is usable, but will give you very short overhead casts: remember, you can only shoot line as long as a loop is rolling forward. With a 6.5 meter belly, you will run out of upper line quickly and the cast will stretch too early and descend toward the water.

Belly D is rather long, but if you can manage to keep it flying, it will offer you some long casting. However, your backcast has to be free of any obstacles and your cast requires perfect timing.

For overhead casting, belly B is probably the best choice of the four. It is a bit too light, but working faster and harder with the rod will compensate. The poorest choice would be the rather heavy belly C, because it would overload the rod, giving you casts with very open loops as shown in the illustration below.

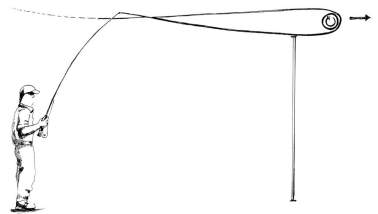

Figure 3-6. Casting belly A, B, or D: narrow loop.

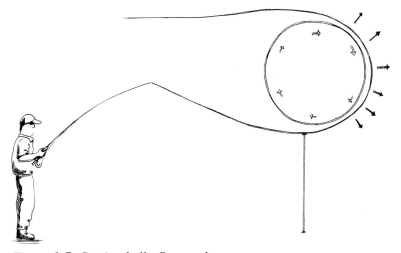

Figure 3-7. Casting belly C: open loop.

For the Scandinavian Spey cast, the length of the belly is most critical, and performing a successful Spey cast is impossible if you don't have the necessary length to form a dynamic loop. This means that short belly A is the least probable candidate in the batch of four (figure 3-8). Bellies B and C both have enough length, but for Spey casting, the line can be a bit heavier. Belly C is therefore be the best option; belly B, which is a bit too light, would be considerably harder to work with.

Long belly D would work for Spey casting, even though it takes up quite a lot of space (and if you are in a position where a Spey cast is needed, space behind you is normally limited). If room for casting is available, the shorter, but rather heavy belly C is still be a better option because it allows you a more concealed position from the spot you are fishing (see figure 3-9).

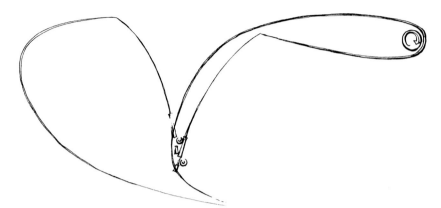

Figure 3-9. Casting belly B, C, or D: With a long loop, you get the characteristic D-shaped loop in the backcast, giving you a fine forward cast.

The four bellies shown draw a clear picture of the principles behind the choice of a belly with the correct length *and* weight.

Running lines

A stubborn myth persists that you can cast better with a thin running line. This myth may be connected to the fact that a thin line gives you a considerably longer cast when you cast a lure on a spinning rod. It is true in this situation that a switch to a thinner nylon line will increase length instantly. Competition casters also use the same kind of nylon used for spin fishing in order to achieve the longest possible cast. But they don't care if the line lands in a heap, as long as the heap lands farther away than the next competitor's.

In practical fishing, your goal is entirely different. You want to control in the cast and give a precise presentation of the fly, preferably in such a way that it lands at the end of a stretched leader. Thin nylon running lines are useless here. A closer look at the function of the running line in the cast and during fishing shows why coated running lines are the best choice.

The running line has two functions in the cast. First, it is a precondition for shooting any line at all. The second concerns the physics of fly casting. The resistance on the lower line comes from the shooting line in two different ways: the running line has its own weight, which is pulled down by gravity and gives lift resistance; and friction resistance occurs when the line passes through the guides on the rod. These resistant forces, put together, adjust the speed of the lower line, making the wheel roll forward and presenting the fly at the end of a stretched leader.

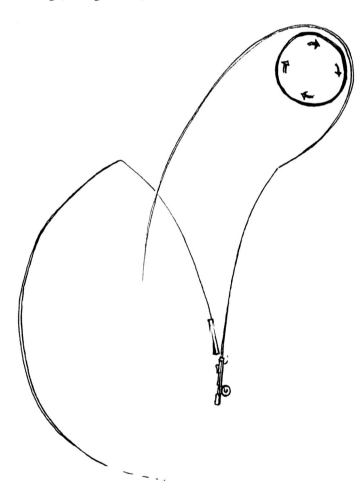

Figure 3-8. Casting belly A: The line is too short for Spey casting and a dynamic loop is impossible to make. In the forward cast, the line is a given a direction upward instead of forward.

Casting with a double-handed rod: You can control the loose line with your left hand in order to make sure it shoots out effort-lessly in the next cast.

With a thin monofilament running line, the accumulated resistance is too small, requiring that you force the wheel forward by adjusting the leader to make it lighter. You could choose a thin and thereby light leader, but it won't be able to transport the fly forward. The other option is to tie on a really short leader, but it may spook shy fish—and short leaders are basically useless for Spey casting. In short, it is impossible to gain 100 percent control of the cast with a monofilament running line.

In practical fishing, the running line carries an important function as well. When you retrieve the fly, you do so by pulling the running line. This is the case when you pull the line to get ready for a new cast after the fly has fished through on a river or stream. The same applies when you fish the shore or in a lake, where you have no current to give the flies lifelike movements; your steady pull of the line creates the illusion of life.

It can be hard to keep your grip on a thin running line with cold and wet hands because it has a tendency to slip between your fingers. This disadvantage turns devastating if it happens the moment the take comes and you raise the rod to set the hook. A coated running line, on the other hand, is easy to handle, even with clammy hands on a cold fall day. Basically, the ability of the line to work well in practical fishing is more important than its cast ability, even if those two can be compatible.

So don't rely on monofilament running line as a shortcut to a longer fly cast. If you want to learn how to cast a long way and still be able to present the fly sensibly, practice and well-balanced tackle are the keys. A running line capable of stretching the leader on all distances is a good starting point because a stretched leader, during most forms of fishing, will increase your effective casting length by 3–6 meters.

Bottom line: use a coated running line in combination with loose bellies (shooting heads). The running line is no more than a level fly line.

If you decide to use a running line, choose one with a suitable diameter—not the thinnest one—to give you the longest casts. My recommendations for running lines for different line classes are shown in the table below.

Line class	diameter (inches/mm)
Single-handed 5/6/7	0.027"/0.69 mm
Single-handed 7/8/9	0.029"/0.74 mm
Double-handed 7/8/9	0.033"/0.84 mm
Double-handed 9/10/11	0.037"/0.94 mm

Notice that line weights under class 5 are not mentioned in the table. The reason is that a straight weight-forward line will serve you better for the lightest fly fishing.

Leader and fly

A good leader is essential for a well-executed fly cast and to get the fly into the right spot. When you use different sizes of flies, the leader is used to adjust the overall line system and keep it in perfect balance.

A featherwing fly size 10 will, under normal circumstances, force you to use a longer leader than a bushy hairwing size 6. The bigger fly also needs to be presented on a heavier leader to get the presentation right.

Things can quickly go awry if you do not realize the importance of the leader in the overall line system. Take the following story as an example.

In the story below, every time I changed my fly and tied on another, I cut off a piece of the leader. When you do that four or five times, the leader will be so much shorter that its length affects the way it behaves in the cast.

By analyzing the cast, you can see that the mass of the upper line is lessened when the leader is shortened. The mass of the lower line, in the form of friction and lift-resistance, and the actual weight of the line are not changed. Because the upper line is lighter, its speed increases compared to the lower line in the forward cast: the cast stretches earlier, and when it is stretched, it descends. If you try to cast longer by increasing the drift and acceleration, the cast will stretch out more or less to the same place, but the extra force will make the fly bounce back and land in a pile of line and leader.

Remember that the cast is changed every time you make your leader longer or shorter, or change to a bigger or smaller fly. I stress the importance of fly and leader in relation to the balance of the cast often: a deeper understanding of these relations can change people's casting skills more dramatically than anything else.

When fly casting goes amiss

Spring has come and a day's fishing for sea trout on the shore is on the schedule. I have checked the fly tackle for shore fishing in advance and tied on a brand-new, shop-bought, clear monofilament tapered leader—I'm as ready as I can ever be. I arrive on the shoreline, and a home-tied fly for sea trout size 6 called Magnus is tied onto the leader. It is a pattern that I have found works well in April, when the sea trout start to roam the shallows in search of prey. I quietly fish the shore, full of pent-up excitement and confidence in what I am doing—besides, I have a proven fish-magnet at the end of the leader. The casts fly out effortlessly, but nothing much happens. After an hour or so, another angler appears, we start talking, and the talk, like so many times before, is directed toward the issue of the right fly for the day. The stranger stubbornly claims that my grayish-brown fly is the wrong choice entirely. Considering the previous hour without fish, he may have a point. From what he is saying, he sounds like he is experienced. He moves on along the shore, while I pick out a tiny hackle fly in screaming orange.

After some time fishing without any contacts, the doubt begins to spread in my mind. The certainty I had when I started has evaporated, and I am almost losing faith altogether. Maybe the reason is that I am fishing with someone else's favorite, and not my own! The Orange Menace is quickly snipped off and the Magnus goes back on. If there is a sea trout out there, the tantalizingly moving Magnus will do the trick, no doubt about that!

Another angler appears on the shore, and as I turn to see if it is a familiar face, I spot the two shining sea trout weighing him down. It may be worth the while to take a break and hear where he caught the two handsome bars of silver. After a short conversation, a bite of Danish pastry and some warm coffee as bribery, I manage to tease out that he has caught the fish farther down the shore at a prominent reef jetting out from shore. He is on his way home, he says, and with that hands over the fly that the two fine fish fell for.

When he has cleared the cliff, I head directly for the reef, tie on his fly, and start fishing. Random thoughts swirl through your head when you send out one cast after another. I start reflecting on the stupidity of what I am doing: I am trying to catch the same two trout, which have long since been caught and probably already rest nice and cold in the freezer at the lucky angler's house. Even if the somewhat clumsily tied fly worked like a lucky charm for him, it obviously doesn't work for me.

I wade ashore, pull up my backpack and head for a spot that has not been fished at all throughout the morning. The tried and tested Magnus goes onto the leader, and when I let go of the line on the first cast, I can feel that something is amiss. I quickly lift the line for another cast, do a couple of false casts, and send the line flying again. Curiously enough, my casts are much shorter now than they were when I started out in the morning, even though the same fly is back on the leader. Besides, the leader doesn't stretch properly, like it should. It merely lands in a big pile, even if I put all my strength behind the casting.

Maybe you already guessed what went wrong?

Every time you change the fly, the leader gets shorter. Once in a while, the leader needs to be restored to its original length. Petit Cascapédia, Canada.

Extend or shorten the leader

The fly and the leader in combination constitute the mass controlling the speed of the upper line in the forward cast. In my work as a tackle designer, I have experimented in order to understand what mass a leader should have if the aim is a nice stretch on short and long casts alike. At the waterside, telling if the leader is too short or too long compared to the fly at the end of the leader is quite a challenge. Let's look at a couple of examples.

If the line tends to stretch faster than it should in the forward cast, and, given the energy you put into the cast, you feel that the fly should go farther than it actually does, the cause is a leader that is too short compared to the size of fly (figure 3-10). This fault is also apparent from the leader's tendency to bounce back after the line stretches. You cannot increase the length of the cast by forcing the tackle. Instead, you have to extend the leader to slow down the upper line,

which means that the lower and upper line are closer to the same speed. The line will stretch farther out, but the upper line still has to be the fastest for the cast to stretch.

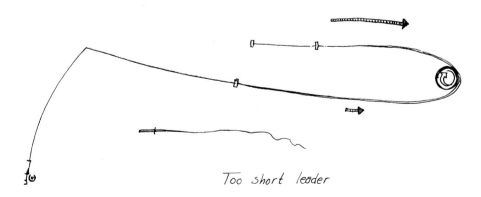

Too short leader

Figure 3-10. If the leader is too short, it will bounce back in the forward cast.

The opposite can also occur: the line does not stretch properly and descends with the leader, landing in a big pile. The trouble here is that the mass of the leader and fly is too large. The long leader causes the upper line to lose speed, before the leader has unrolled and the line is stretched as shown in Figure 3-11.

In order to solve this problem, you have to shorten your leader and remove some of the mass that is slowing the speed of the upper line. With a shorter and thus lighter leader, the speed of the upper line increases. When the upper line moves faster than the lower line in the forward cast, the line will stretch like it should, as shown in the illustrations below.

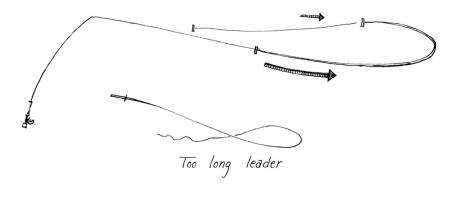

Too long leader

Figure 3-11

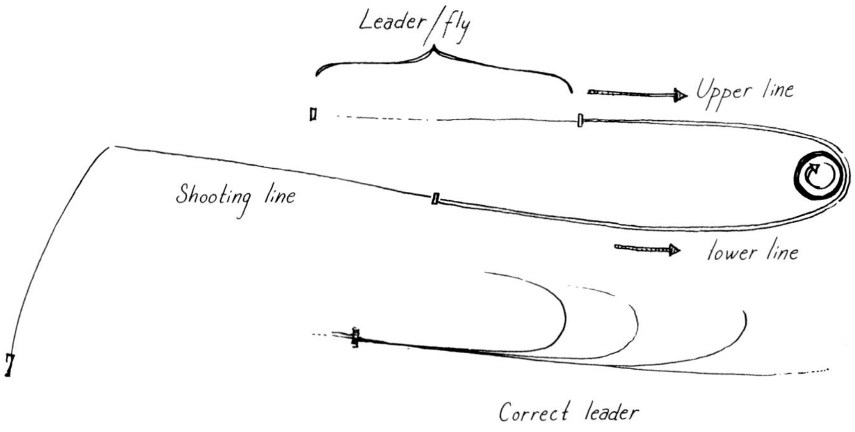

Leader/fly

Upper line

Shooting line

lower line

Correct leader

Figure 3-12

The principal requirement for the leader is to lead the speed of the upper line in the forward cast (read more in chapter 1). The leader, along with the fly, works as a brake on the forward cast. The result is a slower turn of the wheel, which means that it can keep rolling for a longer period.

The leader rests on the water surface in Spey casting, which makes it possible to form a loop without stretching the line behind the caster.

The properties of the leader

Let's look at how to make a leader that effectively balances the line system and yet works well in practical fishing.

No too long ago, fly fishers routinely tied their own leaders out of pieces of nylon with different diameters. But tiny spools of leader do not come cheap, and because the process requires a lot of spools, it quickly became costly. In addition, achieving the same even tapering as that found on leaders bought from a shop was next to impossible.

Today, the most common leader is a ready-made tapered monofilament leader or polyleader (see figure 3-13). An important property in a leader, regardless of type, is the tapering, which ensures that speed is reduced from the line before the fly lands on the water. In practice, the tapering is somewhat of a compromise; the leader should stretch easily on the water, yet the turnover should be adequately subtle to avoid a splash that would spook the fish.

The coarseness of the leader is important in relation to the presentation of the fly. The leader should steer the fly and neither be too thin nor too thick. A large fly will hang awkwardly at the end of a thin leader, and with a leader too thick, a small fly will lose its lively play in the water, ending up like a lifeless lump of feather and hair.

The leader, and particularly the tip of the leader, acts as an invisible link between the fly and the fly line. Make sure, however, that you still tie powerful leaders so you have no excuses during that fight with the really big fish you succeeded in hooking. There is no sport in using light leaders. The fragile tackle increases the risk of losing the fish and prolonging the fight more than necessary.

If the line can carry it, use a powerful leader on a light rod. If conditions allow, a light rod can tire a big fish just as easy as a heavy rod.

A fresh and strong leader can take more abuse than a thin one. For late-season salmon and sea-trout fishing, a time when many would like to release colored fish, the leader should be suitably heavy. The same goes for catch-and-release streams. A released fish that fought too long has a smaller chance of survival because of lactic acid accumulated in its muscles during the fight. The leader should also be heavy when fishing a boulder-strewn river or a weedy stream where it can be weakened by hang-ups and friction from stones.

Therefore, choose the strongest possible leader that will still give you a delicate presentation of the fly in question—in the cast as well as in the actual fishing.

Monofilament leaders

Monofilament leaders are easy to stretch, settle on the water in a straight line, and can be used not only for lighter nymph and dry-fly fishing, but also for shore fishing and, under certain conditions, salmon fishing.

The monofilament leaders I use are tapered, ready-made leaders, described in the table to the right. They are fine for both Spey casting and overhead casting.

Always remember to stretch monofilament leaders thoroughly before use. The slight heat from the friction when you pull the leader through the palm of your hand is enough to straighten it simply and effectively. Also, soak the leader thoroughly before use so it picks up some moisture, making it behave like it should from the first cast. (You can read about attaching leaders to fly lines in chapter 10.)

The table to the right is read in the following way: If your rod is single-handed, 8 ½ feet, and class 6-7, you need a leader of 13 feet. For a double-handed rod, 12 feet, class 8-9, you need 15 feet of leader.

Leaders come in many colors: transparent, green, blue, smoke-colored…. Choose a leader for the water that you are about to fish. Many rivers and streams are tea-colored, for example, because the water runs through peaty marsh. In such a case, a leader with a slight coloration will work, because it is less shiny underwater than a leader as clear as glass.

Single-handed rods	Rod length	Line class	Leader length	Butt diameter	Tippet diameter
Steelhead	8'-10'6	7-9	13'-15'	0.023"	0.012"
Browns and rainbows	8'-9'6	5-7	12'-14'	0.022"	0.010" (1X)
Brookies	7'-9'6	3-5	9'-12'	0.021"	0.007" (4X)

Double-handed rods	Rod length	Line class	Leader length	Butt diameter	Tippet diameter
Coarse	14'-16'	10-11	19'-22'	0.026"	0.015"
Medium	12'-13'6	8-9	15'-19'	0.026"	0.013"
Fine	11'-12'	7-8	15'-18'	0.024"	0.012"

Monofilament Leaders for Single- and Double-Handed Rods

Figure 3-13. A wide selection of polyleaders and monofilament leaders. Notice that polyleaders are fitted with loops, making it simple to change over to a new and more suitable type if conditions dictate. The nylon leader is connected to the fly line with a needle knot.

A large salmon has taken the dry fly. River Bonaventure, Canada.

To show how leaders are tapered differently, several different types of polyleaders and nylon leaders are presented in figure 3-13. The leader has a thick end that is connected to the fly line, but it quickly tapers down, gradually thinning almost to the tip.

The powerful butt end of the leader ensures that the transmission of power from fly line to leader is as direct as possible. The transmission part is not long because coarse materials are quite stiff, regardless of the material used. A suitable length for the thick transmission part should be about one-fifth of the overall length; after this point, the leader should thin out conically toward the tip. The tapering constitutes the largest part of the overall length of the ready-made leader, while the tip is quite short. The leader is meant to be fitted with an extra tip, which is adjusted to the line class, rod length, and fly size in question.

The leader package will often contain advice on how long this tip part should be; it varies for different sizes of flies. Still, it is important to be able to figure out if the leader needs to be longer or shorter. A great deal of experimentation is the way to get that knowledge.

The leader tip must not affect the movements of the fly negatively, meaning that it should be neither too thin nor too thick. You must also remember that the leader tip needs to have enough mass to turn the fly over at the end of the cast.

Lengthening or shortening the leader to turn it into a natural extension of the fly line is indeed a balancing act. Getting it right, however, will make it stretch perfectly, delivering the fly with a discreet plop at the outermost tip.

Polyleaders

Polyleaders are constructed from a monofilament core covered in a flexible polymer coating. The leaders are tapered (honed down) and their rear end is fitted with an eye. The thin end is finished with a nylon tip or a loop to connect the leader tip.

In order to avoid cutting off too much of the ready-made leader, make a surgeon's loop in the thin end of the polyleader. This loop allows you to attach the leader tip to the polyleader with the loop-to-loop principle. (See page 178.)

The tables below include recipes for ready-to-go polyleaders. Here's an example: Say you are going fishing (for sea trout maybe) on the shore with a 9-foot single-handed fly rod class 7/8 and have purchased a polyleader with a diameter of 0.28 mm at the tip. You normally use smaller flies, the biggest ones ranging to a size 6 single hook. The table on the polyleader package says you need a 50 cm long middle section of 0.28 nylon and a tip section of 140 cm with a diameter of 0.24 mm. Now, take approximately 50 cm of 0.28 nylon, make a surgeon loop in one end, and connect the nylon piece with the loop on the polyleader. This middle section acts as a transmission part from the polyleader to the thinner tip. After this, tie a 70 cm piece of 0.26 nylon to the 0.28 mm middle section with a surgeon loop. Finally, tie a 70 cm tip section of 0.24 line to the 0.26 line with a surgeon's knot or a double blood knot (see chapter 10 for more on knots for the fly fisher).

Polyleaders for single-handed rods

Rod	Polyleader	Monofilament joint	Fly size	Tippet diameter
8'–9'6" Class 5/6	5' intermediate or 4' sinking	16" of 0.010" (1X)	Normal Larger flies	24" of 0.009" (2X) + 28" of 0.007" (4X) 24" of 0.009" (2X)
8'–9'6" Class 6/7	6' intermediate or 5' sinking	16" of 0.011" (0X)	Normal Larger flies	24" of 0.010" (1X) + 28" of 0.009" (2X) 24" of 0.010" (1X)
9'–10' Class 7/8	7' intermediate or 5' sinking	20" of 0.011" (0X)	Normal Larger flies	28" of 0.010" (1X) + 28" of 0.009" (2X) 28" of 0.010" (1X)
9'–10' Class 8/9	8' intermediate or 6' intermediate	31" of 0.012"	Normal Larger flies	39" of 0.010" (1X) 24" of 0.011" (0X)

Polyleaders for double-handed rods

Rod	Polyleader	Monofilament joint	Fly size	Tippet diameter
11'–12' Class 7/8	9' intermediate or 7' sinking	20" of 0.013"	Normal Larger flies	24" of 0.011" (0X) + 28" of 0.010" (1X) 20" of 0.012"
12'–13'4" Class 8/9	10' intermediate or 8' sinking	20" of 0.014"	Normal Larger flies	24" of 0.012" + 28" of 0.011" (0X) 20" of 0.013"
13'2"–14'1" Class 9/10	13' intermediate or 10' sinking	24" of 0.015"	Normal Larger flies	47" of 0.013" 24" of 0.014"
15'–16' Class 10/11	14' intermediate or 10' sinking	28" of 0.016"	Normal Larger flies	59" of 0.014" 28" of 0.015"

Between polyleader and leader tip, a middle section from slightly heavier nylon is added to avoid cutting the polyleader when the leader tip is changed.

Figure 3-14. The characteristics of the polyleader are signaled by its color. Transparent means slow sink; brown, fast sink; and black, extra fast sink.

As you change a fly, the 0.24 tip is gradually shortened and, at some point in time, you will have to tie on a new piece of 0.24 mm at the end of the leader. Because this new piece is tied to the middle section, which is made from 0.26 mm line, you avoid cutting and shortening the ready-made leader. Change the middle section when it becomes worn.

This middle section is a great advantage when you change flies or shorten or extend the leader tip often.

Polyleader—a leader with many assets

When polyleaders were brought to market in the 1990s, most of them were quite short (around 5 feet) and made of thin monofilament cores fashioned from a stiff material, which meant that the coating had a tendency to crack off. Today, however, these problems have been fixed, and polyleaders come in a range of different lengths in durable materials. Fly

fishers, in running as well as still waters, have adopted these leaders readily, and they are now almost as widely used as monofilament leaders for a couple of very good reasons:

- *The tapering of the polyleader makes it a natural extension of the fly line, which gives you a gradual and even transmission of energy all the way to the fly*
- *The considerable weight of the leader itself means that it stretches well*
- *Polyleaders with different densities make it easy to present the fly in different depths*

I am very satisfied with polyleaders, mainly because they are excellent for close-distance fishing due to their weight. This is especially true when you work a double-handed rod where the long monofilament leaders previously made it an impossible affair to fish distances less than 10 meters. With polyleaders, you can cast and fish effectively with just a couple of meters of fly line and the leader outside the tip guide.

The leader decides the fishing depth

Figure 3-14 shows a collection of polyleaders: an intermediate (transparent), a fast sinking (brown), and a super fast sinking (black). I find this selection adequate because a greater variation in fishing depth is better handled by changing the belly to one with a different density. In the table below, you can see how fast leaders descend through the water.

Model	Sink rate
I – *Intermediate (neutral)*	*3 cm per second*
FS – *Fast sinking*	*8 cm per second*
SFS – *Super Fast Sinking*	*13 cm per second*

The thick end of the polyleader is fitted with an eye, meaning that the fly line also has to be fitted with an integrated loop (see chapter 10 for more on knots for the fly fisher). Connecting the loop on the polyleader to the loop at the end of the fly line makes connecting and disconnecting the fly line and leader an easy task when you are fishing, meaning that you can easily switch leaders according to the conditions. Don't forget to stretch a polyleader fresh from the pack before you start fishing to ensure that it behaves optimally in the cast and during fishing.

Choice of leader

Which leader should you choose: monofilament or polyleader? Depending on the fishing situation, I change between the two. As a general rule, I always use polyleaders for salmon fishing and only change to a monofilament leader to use a technique called a riffling hitch (see pages 34–37) and to dry-fly fish.

Also for regular wet-fly fishing in class 2–6, a monofilament leader is preferable because it gives you a more delicate presentation, if the fly is at the end of a long, thin nylon leader.

For shore fishing for sea trout, I use both poly- and nylon leaders. For light shore fishing, class 6–7, a monofilament leader works well with smaller flies. A polyleader, on the other hand, is better for shore and pike fishing with heavier single-handed rods because it takes more power transmission on a long line to turn over the leader with a large fly at its end.

Figure 3-15. The nylon leader to the left is perfect for the light approach, while the polyleader on the right is versatile and can handle large flies and long casts, yet allows you to fish close in as well.

The role of the leader in the overhead cast is to act as a brake on the upper line, and both leaders can execute this task. In practice, the resistance comes from two sources: The actual weight of the leader and wind resistance. Below are two different leaders that are, in practice, suitable for the same rod, line, and fly, but each is constructed in a different way.

The upper leader is a tapered monofilament leader measuring 5.2 meters, while the lower one is a somewhat shorter intermediate polyleader. Assume that the same type and size of fly is meant to go on each leader. Length and thickness of the recommended tip for each leader is stated in the table below.

Leader type	Name of ready-made leader	Recommended tippet
Monofilament	Heavy Salmon (17'1 with 0.015" tip)	39" of 0.014" + 47" of 0.013"
Polyleader	MWF Twohand 9/10 Intermediate (14'5 with 0.018" tip)	24" of 0.015" + 47" of 0.013"

As mentioned, two different resistances work on the upper line. The first comes from the actual weight of the leader, which is affected by gravity. The other resistance is due to the surface area of the leader, which meets friction on its way through the air. In order to make the discussion more specific, I have given measurements for each of the leaders, including the tip. The weight of the leader tip is calculated from the density of the monofilament leader, which is 1.21 g/3 cm.

Leader type	Length (inches)	Weight (grains)	Volume (cubic inches)	Surface area (square inches)
Monofilament	205	19.6	0.064	1.98
Polyleader	173	43.2	0.131	2.62
Recommended tippet				
Monofilament	87	3.7	0.012	1.15
Polyleader	71	3.1	0.010	0.95
Ready-made leader and recommended tippet				
Monofilament	291	23.3	0.076	3.13
Polyleader	244	46.3	0.140	3.58

A salmon took the dry fly in the last light of day. Petit Cascapédia, Canada.

As shown, the monofilament leader plus tip is 120 centimeters longer than the polyleader, but the polyleader is twice as heavy. The volume is also double that of the monofilament leader while the difference in surface area is far less: the polyleader is a mere 14 percent larger than the monofilament leader.

The resistance of the monofilament leader primarily comes from air resistance. Roughly estimated, about 85 percent of the resistance is due to air friction, while only 15 percent is from the weight of the leader. The distribution for the polyleader may be 75 percent from weight and 25 percent from air friction. To explain further: a long monofilament leader has a low weight of its own and therefore is unstable in the air, which means that air resistance gets higher. Conversely, the actual weight of the polyleader is higher, and it therefore flies more true in the air, which means less air friction. This contrast is shown in the illustrations below.

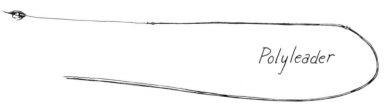

The nylon leader gives higher air resistance.

Figure 3-16. The weight of the polyleader makes it fly in a more stable way through the air.

The long monofilament is usable for long casting, but the transmission of energy is poor, causing the leader to collapse. So it is almost impossible to cast on a short line, especially with a double-handed rod, because you need to have almost the whole belly through the guides. If you add the length of the belly to the length of the rod and leader, you come up with the shortest possible casting length, which is around 20 meters, measured from the foot of the caster to where the fly lands. That's quite a bit.

In comparison, you can cast a very short line if you use a polyleader: casting lengths less than 10 meters are uncomplicated. You'll have excellent fly control on a short line, and

even in longer casts, the fly has more direct contact with a polyleader. The polyleader is simply superior for stretching the leader, due to its high mass, which ensures the best possible transmission of power.

Leaders for fishing with sinking lines

Fishing with sinking lines can be effective, but a careful adjustment of the leader is necessary. A certain amount of resistance in the leader is needed to get a reasonable casting length and stable casting. But if you use an ordinary monofilament leader, it will have to be long enough to get the resistance needed, which means that presentation goes out of the equation. The problem with sinking lines and long leaders is shown below: the sinking line descends without pulling the nylon leader with it to the fish.

Figure 3-17. A long nylon leader will not present the fly to the fish properly.

I once tried to solve this problem by using two flies on a shorter leader as shown in figure 3-18. But the weight and air resistance from the two flies meant that the length of the leader had to be considerably shorter. The benefit, however, is that two flies on the leader will allow you to experiment. Using two flies on the leader is not permitted everywhere though, and in small weedy streams, it is difficult to handle.

Figure 3-18. Two flies on the leader will pull the nylon leader down more easily.

Sinking polyleaders are the perfect solution for fishing with sinking lines. With just one fly on the leader you can get the resistance on the upper line you need for the cast and still present the fly in the right depth, as shown in figure 3-19.

Figure 3-19. A sinking polyleader with a short nylon tip is the best solution for fishing with sinking lines.

In figure 3-20 the advantages of polyleaders for sinking-line fishing are clear: A short leader is needed for a deep presentation, but a short monofilament leader (top drawing) creates very little resistance on the upper line. In this scenario, the wheel will rotate faster, ruling out the possibility of a long cast. In the bottom illustration, a sinking polyleader with a short monofilament nylon tip is shown. This setup has more resistance due to its higher weight, and a fine presentation and long cast are still a possibility.

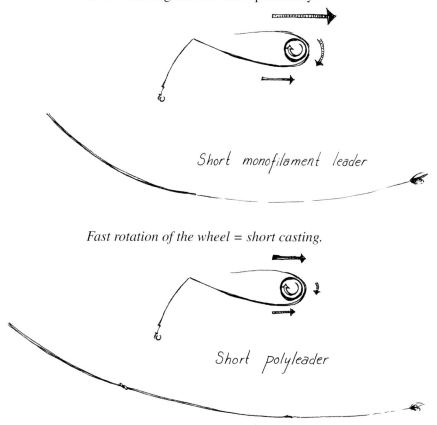

Short monofilament leader

Fast rotation of the wheel = short casting.

Short polyleader

Figure 3-20. Slow rotation of the wheel = longer casting.

Casting practice with a piece of wool yarn on the leader

At the end of the fly line and leader is the fly, and I have mentioned several times that the length and thickness is adapted to the fly in fishing and casting alike. But what about casting practice on a lawn? You often see people practicing in dry conditions with nothing at the end of the leader—and sometimes with no leader at all. Unfortunately, they will adopt a range of misconceptions about casting. To make your land practice worthwhile, you need a suitable leader at the end of the line.

The resistance from the fly at the end of the leader is important; even if the fly is just a tiny one, the effect is unmistakable. Casting with and without a fly at the end of the leader are two entirely different things—and if you doubt this, try it for yourself.

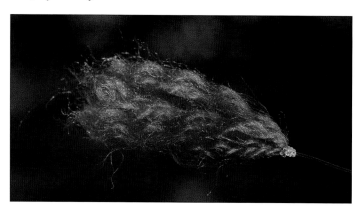

Figure 3-21. A piece of wool yarn works fine as a fly when you practice casting.

When you cast on grass, use a dummy. Some fishermen use a worn-out fly with the hook-bend nipped off, but a better solution is to make a small woolly dummy as shown in the photo above. Take a short piece of wool yarn and fold it once. Next, tie the yarn to the end of the leader with a blood knot and trim the ends of the yarn with a pair of scissors, reducing the length of the wool as desired. The more powerful the rod you use is, the bigger the woolly yarn fly should be; it has to represent the wind resistance and weight from a bigger fly normally found at the end of the leader on a heavy rod.

For a single-handed rod class 6/7, double the yarn once and trim it to a length of about 1 centimeter. For a double-handed rod class 8/9, a 2-centimeter piece of yarn doubled two or three times is suitable.

Use a high-visibility color such as red or orange so you can keep track of where the dummy fly lands and check if the leader stretches properly.

An angler's dreams are made of "silver" like this perfect salmon from the Grand Cascapédia, Canada.

Chapter 4
Overhead Casting with a Single-Handed Rod

In the magical light of sunset, the sea trout leaves the deep parts of the river. Perhaps it can be tempted with the right fly fished near the tailwater of the pool. Rio Grande, Argentina.

The fly fisher's basic cast

This chapter deals with overhead casting on the single-handed rod. If you are still inexperienced with fly casting, or perhaps you need fine-tuning of the basic techniques of fly casting, start your training here. The simple overhead cast is the foundation for all subsequent casting and is often called the basic cast.

Even the experienced fly caster may benefit from studying the basic cast, because a good understanding makes it easier to grasp the instructions for all the casts developed from the principles of this cast. If you have trouble with the more advanced casts, return to the basic cast: learn it and make sure, through practice, that you are executing it correctly.

Toward the end of the chapter, you'll see how you can push your cast to greater distances by actively using the wrist and underarm and working on the position of your feet.

Casting practice on grass

The basic cast can be practiced on a lawn. Pull out line from the reel to equal two rod lengths plus the leader, which should be a regular tapered nylon leader.

The basic cast meets reality

In the basic cast, start with the line straight in front of you. This cast works perfectly on a big, flat lawn with room for a backcast. But the basic cast in its purest form is rarely used in practical fishing. Trees and bushes often make an extra high backcast necessary. And in running water, you will likely have to change the direction of the line before it is lifted to send it back out at another angle.

The basic cast consists of several positions and movements between these positions. "Positions" refers to the points the rod moves to or from during the different phases of the cast. The movements are your own movements of the arm, leading the rod back and forth through the different positions. (Read more about the positions and the physics of the loop in chapter 1.) This chapter deals with your movements: moving the fly cast off of paper and into reality.

The basic cast is critical. In fact, it does not make any sense to start on other types of casts before you master the basic cast.

People with many years of fly casting behind them may find it pointless to practice the basic cast with only a few meters of fly line beyond the tip guide. But in my experience, even seasoned casters should practice the basic cast once in a while.

Accurate movements and precise timing are essential in a long cast. Small deviations cause big failures. In a short cast, however, things look different. You can do a clumsy cast and still make the line stretch tolerably. If you are happy enough to cast a short line with limited precision, there's no need for intensive casting practice. But if your ambition is to cast farther with great precision and ultimately reach the kind of freedom you get from being able to adjust your casts and place the fly during many different conditions, then the key is to practice the basic cast to perfection. A thoroughly memorized basic cast is a precondition for a long day of effective and concentrated fishing.

The phases of the basic cast

The basic cast is divided into two phases: the backcasting movement and the forward cast.

Focus on a good backcast

The hardest phase is dealing with the backward movements: once you make a perfect backcast, sending the line flying in a good forward cast is relatively simple. However, a cast is hard to correct if it starts with a bad backcast.

Style, rod handling, and grip

Controlled movements are important in all kinds of fly casts. Casting with sloppy or sudden, quick movements is a sign that the caster is not in control. The caster should emanate style and a relaxed attitude at all times. The calmer you are when you cast, the more energy you can focus on the fishing; this is the first lesson on the basic cast.

It is essential to lead the rod in a straight line back and forth in the basic cast. Seen from above, the tip guide should follow a straight line. If the tip guide follows a curved course, the rod has moved outside the vertical line of casting, which will result is a less effective cast. Remember, however, that the line always follows the movements of the tip guide, so it is important to hold the rod slightly inclined outward. Otherwise, the line will collide with the rod as it loses altitude during the front and backcast due to gravity.

Style, as well as casting plane, is easier to control if you hold the handle correctly. (Refer to chapter 2 for more about the correct hand grip.) Keep your the wrist locked and make sure that only the shoulder and upper arm deliver the force to drive the rod, so the powers of the rod are utilized in the best possible way and a better and more controlled cast is achieved.

Think of the arm as having three hinges: wrist, elbow joint, and shoulder joint. The joints in the elbow and shoulder are best suited for forceful movements, while the wrist takes care of the finer adjustments. To start, though, strive to cast without bending your wrist.

The backcast consists of three movements

While it is tempting to say that the backcast is more important than the forward cast, one thing is certain: A good backcast is the precondition for a good forward cast.

The backward casting movements are often described as the backcast, but it is important to underline that we speak of three movements in the basic cast, not just one. You could correctly speak of the backward movements, but in practice it is easier to speak of a backcast only.

> The backcast is performed by carrying out three movements following each other: the lift, the actual backcast, and the drift.

The lift is the movement from starting position to the front stop. This movement is steady and very slow. The lift is now followed by the actual backcast (from this point on, simply called the backcast), which is the movement from the front stop to the back stop: this movement is gradually accelerating. The final movement is the drift. This is the movement from the back stop to the back position. The drift is an even and rather slow movement.

The three movements are shown collectively in figure 4-1. In the first stage, the line is lifted to the front stop in such a way that it draws an almost even line from the tip guide to the leader, which is still clinging to the surface of the water.

Now, the backcast begins. The movement is illustrated in the drawing by two dotted lines. The rod is stopped in an early back stop, and the straight line going from tip guide to the line end causes the backcast to send the line straight back.

At this point, the drift toward the back position is initiated (the rod to the far left), which is actually just a controlled lift of the rod in readiness for the forward cast as soon as the line is stretched out.

Notice that the four fishing rods in the illustration correspond to the rod at different phases of the cast. The two solid-line rods are the front stop and back position.

In order to move the rod from the starting position to the front stop, the lift is made. Between the front stop and the back stop, the backcast is made. The movements backward are finished with the drift, which follows immediately after the backcast reaches the back stop. In the next sections, each of these three steps will be described in detail.

> The point of the drift, where you follow the rod through, backwards and upwards, is to increase the acceleration the rod makes in the forward cast. The drift is not always the same movement—in a short cast very little drift is made, while longer casts demand a longer drift backwards before the forward cast is initiated.

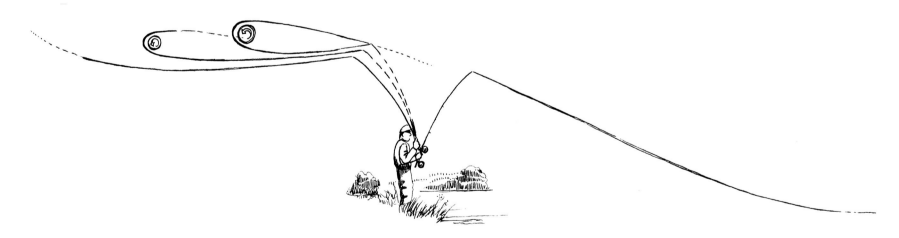

Figure 4-1. The three movements of the overhead cast: the lift, backcast, and drift.

In search of the famous salmon of River Alta in Norway, a place where Spey casting is a must in the upper parts of the river with its steep sites.

The lift

The lift is an extremely important yet overlooked stage in the cast. One of the most important functions of the lift is to bring the line into the right position in relation to the back-cast, which decides the direction of the line when it is thrown back. The better you are at controlling the lift for the back-cast, the better the backcast will be—and thus the forward cast as well.

> At some point, when you launch yourself into new casts, the lift will be what decides if those casts turn out right. Focus on the lift at the start of your career as a fly fisher: the lift is, in short, the key to the successful cast.

The lift is the movement from the starting position to the front stop. The movement with rod and line is shown in fig-ure 4-2. In the starting position before the lift, the rod points downward in a slanting angle, and line and leader are stretched out directly in an extension of the rod. There should be no loose line at all.

The lift to the front stop should happen slowly enough to lift the line but not the leader from the water. It pulls the fly line clear of the water and suspends it in the correct angle before the backcast.

In the backcast the line is sent straight backward, opposite the direction it is pointing on the drawing. This angle slants backward, which is the right direction for a regular overhead cast.

When the line is stretched out behind the caster, it lowers a bit due to gravity. When the forward cast is initiated, the line will hang in a horizontal position or just below. The straight line between the tip guide and the leader is important.

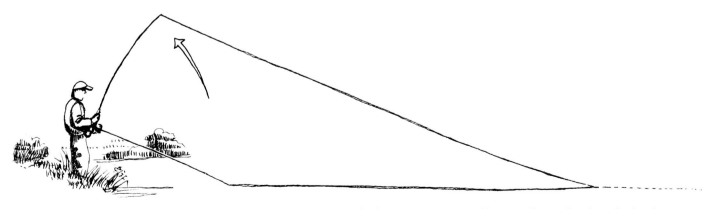

Figure 4-2. The lift from the starting position to the front stop causes the line to position itself in a right angle when the backcast is initiated.

Figure 4-3.

The rod points in the direction of the line in the starting position.

If the fly line is lifted too early, the line overtakes the tip guide too soon, causing you to lose contact with the line. When this happens, the actual backcast will not affect and move the line. With a floating line and a monofilament leader, it's actually hard to do the lift too slowly, as long as there are at least 8-10 meters of line and leader outside the tip guide. This step looks slightly different with sinking lines or fast sinking leaders, but you'll deal with that later on.

The technique involved in the lifting movement for the basic cast is simple. The starting position is shown in figure 4-3, where the rod is pointing in the direction of the line. First, check that the grip is correct and your casting arm is relaxed. Next, bend the wrist to get the correct angle between the fly rod and your underarm. The angle depends on your build, or more precisely, the relationship between your upper and lower arm. So in practice, this angle varies somewhat.

Figure 4-4.

The lift is concluded. The rod is in the front stop. The angle between the lower and upper arms is approximately 90 degrees.

The lift is now performed by simply bending your arm at the elbow joint so your upper and lower arms form a 90-degree angle. The lift is completed, and the rod is in the front stop.

Again, the precise guidelines for the angles in the casting movements are hard to give accurately because no two casters have the same stature and relation between their upper and lower arms. Some people have highly developed upper arms,

and they may find hard to completely close the elbow. Instead, you should focus on the positions of the rod because the rod decides the direction of line in the backcast and helps the lift to come more or less naturally.

Referring to the face of the clock (see the drawing on page 30), the rod should be at 1:30 in the front stop, as shown in figure 4-4.

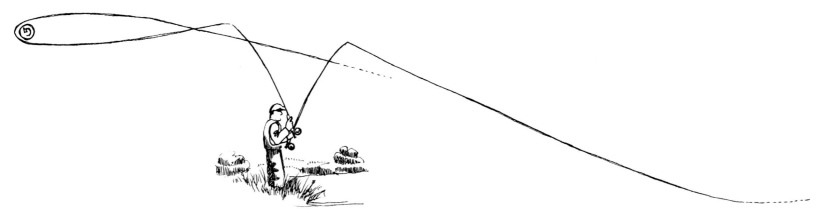

Figure 4-5. In the backcast, the rod is moved from the front stop to the back stop.

The backcast

The actual backcast begins at the front stop and ends at the back stop. The movement is shown with rod and line in figure 4-5. The angle between the front stop and the back stop is typically between 50 and 55 degrees for both short and long casts. The movement between the two positions should be powerful enough to move the line with such speed that it stretches behind you, and the movements should gradually accelerate, which means slow at first, with a gradual increase of speed all the way to the back stop.

In the back stop, a sudden stop occurs and the movement of the rod is almost completely checked, allowing the rod to deliver its energy to the line. At this point, the line will overtake the tip guide and form a loop in the backcast.

The speed of the line must increase continuously from the front stop to the back stop. If the speed decreases, the line will start to pass the tip guide too soon and a large open loop will form in the backcast. If this happens, the line, leader, and fly run the risk of hitting the tip guide on their way backward.

The transition from the lift to the backcast is fluid, because the backcast starts slowly with a gradual acceleration to the momentary stop. During practice, make a pronounced front stop in order to get a better feel for the right time to start speeding up the line.

While you're practicing the basic cast, it is just as beneficial to make a pronounced back stop as well. In practical fishing, you won't accentuate the back stop quite as clearly; it is more a matter of changing the speed on the backward movement.

> During your exercises, it is wise to do overly accentuated movements between the different positions: the exaggeration will help you get a grasp of the fundamentals—you get a better understanding of the dynamics of the cast by exaggerating.

The movement itself in the backcast is relatively simple. The starting position is Figure 4-4, where the lower arm forms a 90-degree angle with the upper arm. By closing the elbow, the rod will end up in the back position as shown in figure 4-6. Notice how the movement for the actual backcast is centered on the elbow: upper arm and lower arm more or less meet without lifting the elbow. Differences in build may mean that you have to change that movement slightly to position the rod correctly.

Figure 4-6. The rod is in the back stop.

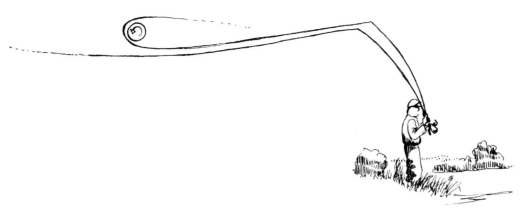

Figure 4-7. From the back stop, the drift is made by moving the rod upward and backward to the back position.

The movement from the back stop to the back position is called the drift. It occurs when the loop is made in the backcast but before the line is stretched out behind the caster. The drift is shown with a rod and line above.

> The drift is made by lifting the elbow, which will lead the rod farther back, increasing the stretch of acceleration in the forward cast. The drift should be made slower than the speed of the upper line; otherwise you will lose contact with the line. The movement is also adjusted in such a way that the drift is completed before the line is stretched out completely behind you.

The length of the cast determines how much the elbow is lifted and consequently how much the line accelerates in the forward cast. The longer the cast, the more speed the line needs, making the drift correspondingly larger.

It is important to understand why the backcast is followed by the drift instead of just taking the rod to the back position. There are two good reasons. The first is that the loop is made in the backcast as a consequence of the difference in heights between the front stop and the back stop, as seen in the direction of the cast. An early back stop will create a narrow loop behind you, which is close to a horizontal plane in the air. If the rod was led directly to the back position, the loop would be correspondingly larger.

The second good reason to complete the drift is that the direction of the line in the backcast is decided by the back stop, combined with the direction of the line during the lift. If the actual backcast is not stopped at an early and high point by an early back stop, the line will fly downward behind the caster instead of straight back. An early back stop is the precondition for a high backcast.

With a high backcast, you will have the reserve needed for a well-aimed forward cast. With a low backcast, however, you run the risk that the fly will never land on the water, but in the bushes or the trees behind you.

It may be necessary for some casters to lift their elbows slightly, particularly casters who have short and very thick upper arms.

The drift

At the end of the backcast, the rod is in the back position. In slightly longer casting, you will need a higher speed on the line for the forward cast. But the angle between the back stop and the front stop does not change in relation to the length of line you need to cast. Instead, the rod is moved from the back stop and then farther backward to the back position. This movement increases the angle to the front stop. You can now accelerate the rod over a longer span, increasing the speed of the line and thus the length of the cast.

The movement of the drift itself is shown in figure 4-8. Note that only the elbow is lifted. How much you lift your elbow depends on the intended length of the cast: longer casts necessitate a bigger drift. But regardless of the type of drift, you must maintain the angle between upper and lower arm, as well as that between the lower arm and fly rod.

Make sure that the rod stays in the back position until the forward cast is initiated. It sounds obvious to not move the rod forward until the forward cast is commenced, but in practice, many fishermen move the rod slightly forward again. When that happens, you lose the extra angle gained with the drift.

The rod is led from the back position to the front stop in the forward cast.

The forward cast

This brings us to the forward cast, which merely consists of a single movement. Compared to the backward casting movements, the forward cast seems simple. Combined with a backcast that is done correctly, it is actually relatively easy to do a good forward cast.

The forward cast is shown in figure 4-9. From the back position, the rod is led to the front stop. As in the backcast, the movement in the forward cast should be gradually accelerating, followed by a sudden stop (deceleration). Don't allow the speed to drop, otherwise the line will overtake the tip guide too early.

The jellyfish principle

To understand the meaning of a gradually accelerating movement followed by a sudden stop, imagine the following scenario: You find a jellyfish on the beach and for some reason,

Figure 4-8. The elbow is lifted in the drift, so that the rod is guided upward and backward to the back position.

known only to yourself, you feel the urge to spear the jelly-fish with a soft flexible stick and send it sailing toward the horizon. It sounds simple, but several things may go wrong in the process:

> **1.** *If the acceleration at the start of the movement is too sudden, the jellyfish will be ripped from the stick and land with a splashing sound behind you.*
> **2.** *If the acceleration is too subtle, the movements are gradual and slow; the jellyfish will be sent flying in a soft arc skyward and lands a few meters farther down the beach.*
> **3.** *If your stop is a sudden jerk, the jellyfish will be torn from the stick and land right in front of your boots.*
> **4.** *But if you can manage a gradually increasing acceleration followed by an appropriate stop, you will manage to send the jellyfish flying in a flat arc, landing on target even at some distance.*

Even though the example may sound silly, it clearly illustrates the "acceleration-stop-movement" you need to aim for in the backcast as well as the forward cast.

The front stop should be a very firm movement in order to create an anchor point for the line. As with the back stop in the backcast, you are dealing with a sudden stop, which is also the case during practical fishing; the stop should be abrupt and firm.

The combination of the accelerating forward cast and the distinct front stop are central to all types of casts. Distinct stop movements should be maintained always, not just during practice on grass.

Another important point to notice is that the rod stays in the front stop toward the end of the forward cast until the line is almost stretched. In practical fishing, however, this is slightly different: you lower the rod as the line unfolds. But, when you first learn this cast, it is important to keep the rod in the front stop position until the line is stretched out completely.

Wrong direction in the forward cast

You can figure out if the front stop and the speed of the forward cast are correct by keeping an eye on where the line lands:

> **1.** *If the front stop is correct and if the speed on the forward cast is adjusted to the length of the line, the whole line will land evenly stretched out before you.*
> **2.** *If the front stop is too low, the loop will be very large; the middle part of the line will land first with the leader and tip part of the line descending afterward.*
> **3.** *If the front stop is too high, the line will hit the tip guide and stop there.*
> **4.** *If the forward cast is made too slowly, the line will not stretch out completely.*
> **5.** *If the forward cast is made too fast, the line will stretch out quickly in the air but bounce back and land in a pile.*

Some of these errors (2, 4, and 5) can actually be used intentionally in practical fishing—dry-fly and nymph fishing, for example—where you often need the line to land in a snake-like curl on the water, giving the fly the opportunity to float along drag free for a while. But you don't want to practice these during basic casting exercises.

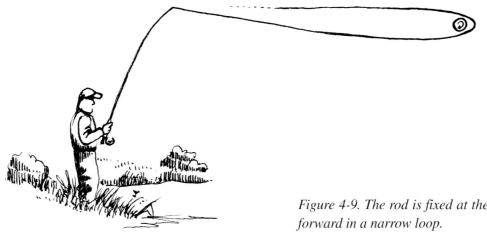

Figure 4-9. The rod is fixed at the front stop. The line flies forward in a narrow loop.

Commercial net fishing has been banned in Iceland since 1933. This visionary policy explains the marvelous salmon fishing on Saga Island. Vest Rangá, vandfaldet Ægisíðufoss.

Figure 4-10. In the forward cast, the elbow is pulled back without opening the elbow angle too much.

The elbow position

The movement of the forward cast is shown in figure 4-10; essentially, the upper arm is pulled down to vertical, almost as if you were elbowing someone in the belly. When you make this movement, the angle between upper and lower arm will automatically open up slightly, returning your upper and lower arm to a right angle. But beware: if you deliberately try to find the right angle, the angle will often open too much. The result will be that the front stop is lowered and the loop is opened.

In fact, it is better to keep the angle closed all the way to the front stop, like you would if you were to elbow someone: the upper arm will then point slightly backward and the tip of the elbow will be visible behind you.

If you open the angle at the elbow, the rod is pushed forward and you do not maximize the potential of the blank. Instead, pull the rod by keeping the angle closed so you use the blank better, especially the lower part of it.

The basic cast in full

Now that you understand the details of the individual movements of the basic cast, it is time to unify the individual steps. The series of photographs on the following pages show you how to execute the basic cast correctly. Every stage of the cast is shown in detail and as a full frame, which will enable you to see the movement of the casting arm, as well as the effect on the rod and line.

In figure 4-11, the line is straight downstream and the caster is about to lift the line for the next cast. Notice the relaxed attitude.

Figure 4-11. Correct grip and relaxed posture.

Figure 4-12. The rod is lifted for the front stop.

Figure 4-13. The rod is moved to the back stop in the backcast.

In figure 4-12, the rod is taken from the starting position to the front stop through the lift.

Notice that the line is hanging in an almost straight line from the tip guide, with the leader still attached to the surface. Also, note that the direction of the cast equals the direction of the backcast.

If the lift is done too quickly or too slowly, the line will hang straight down from the tip guide.

In figure 4-13, the actual backcast is recently completed: the rod has been brought from the front stop to the back stop. If you compare this shot to the previous detail photo, you can see that the elbow has been closed and is brought forward a bit. In the full frame picture, you can see how the rod has stopped and the line is flying backward. Notice the narrow loop made between the front stop and the back stop in the direction of the cast.

Figure 4-14. The drift will lead the rod to the back position. You will now be able to accelerate over a longer stretch in the forward cast.

In figure 4-14, the rod is taken to the back position with a drift, which means that the elbow is lifted a bit. Unlike in the previous detailed photo, the tip of the elbow is now visible in front of the caster. On the large photo below, you will see the line hanging almost horizontally behind the caster; it's now an easy job to send the line forward horizontally in the forward cast.

Figure 4-15. The forward cast is the movement from the back position to the front stop.

Figure 4-15 marks the end of the forward cast: the rod is in the front stop. The tip of the elbow is no longer visible in front of the body and the lower arm is lowered considerably. In the full frame photo, the rod has been stopped. The rod is curving slightly forward. Note how the line is in the process of overtaking the tip guide and a narrow loop is building up. From now on, the line simply rolls out; the rod is not lowered farther.

Figure 4-16. When you stick to and observe the stop positions, the casts will be handsome and effective.

In figure 4-16, the cast is finished. The line descends toward the water. The fishing can begin.

As described in the introduction, the basic cast is a stylized cast, with only limited applicability during practical fishing. Let's take a closer look at which parts of the cast can be changed and adapted for practical fishing and which stages you cannot depart from.

Limitations of the basic cast

The two main limitations of the described basic cast are that direction and length are fixed points. In the basic cast, the line is lifted and sent back in the same direction, which can work very well in a lake or on the shore. But you will often seek to lengthen the cast by shooting line on the other hand. (How to shoot line is described in chapter 6 on single and double haul.)

When you practice the basic cast, the length of the line is fixed (around two rod lengths plus leader), and this could be a line length you could also use for short casts with dry flies and nymphs in a small stream. In such a case, you would change the direction of the line between casts and use the current to fish the fly.

The basic cast in practice

When you start practicing the basic cast, be sure to carry out the movements precisely so you adhere to and clearly mark all the stop positions. In practical fishing, you may accentuate some of these stops a little less to give you a more fluid and harmonious cast.

The first adjustment is the transition from the lift to the backcast. In casting practice, the rod is stopped completely in the front stop, but when this position is memorized, it will be to your advantage to make a more gliding transition between the two movements. Make sure that the lift is still a gradual movement, which will turn into a gradual acceleration the moment the rod passes the front stop. If the acceleration starts too early, the line will move upward instead of directly backward in the backcast.

The lift is the preparation for a gradually accelerating movement, which is stopped at the back stop in the overhead cast. The transition from the actual backcast and to the drift stays the same.

The sudden slowing down during the back stop is perhaps the most important part of the perfect fly cast, and if this stage is softened, the result will be a more open loop. Maintaining the timing of the back stop is therefore of utmost importance.

> **Utilize the drift fully**
> The importance of the drift depends on the length of line you want to cast. In relatively short casts, the drift is not strictly necessary. But in longer casts, where the danger lies in starting the forward cast too early, the drift is absolutely necessary. Many casters have a tendency to start the forward cast very slowly, making the rod almost creep forward. Unfortunately, the effective length of acceleration is thereby reduced. So make sure not to accelerate slowly when initiating the forward cast.

When the rod is in the front stop, the cast is finished, but in practical fishing you still have the phase where the line lands on the water. The principle involved here is that the front stop is still accentuated, but the rod is led toward the water at the same speed as the line's descent through the air (see figure 4-16). The line is stretched perfectly and the fly contact is

Figure 4-17. The whole belly is outside the tip guide with a couple of false casts, and the line can be sent flying again.

direct. Should you inadvertently lower the rod too early, the loop will open too much.

False casting

When you do a longer cast, make a couple of false casts first. To false cast means holding the line in the air in the front and backcast. The purpose is to work more line out through the tip guide, getting the belly (the shooting head) clear of the rod. The line is shot out gradually in the front and backcast. Only when the belly is outside the tip guide can you make the rod work to its potential.

Another good reason for false casting is to place the line optimally and straight behind the rod in the backcast (see the illustration on page 95). With the line hanging straight back and close to horizontal, you will be able to load the rod deeply in the forward cast. The line will be sent flying in a straight line with a minimum loss of energy.

No loose wrists—for a start!

I hope the detailed description of the basic cast has given you a deeper understanding of how to send the line flying with high speed and without strain or using too much energy.

In the initial phase of your practice, it is important to get a sense of how the rod is loaded and unloaded in the best and most powerful way, which means leaving the job to the upper arm and the shoulder.

The movements between the different stop positions may seem a bit mechanized, but they have to be if you want your body to become accustomed to the movements. Otherwise, you run the risk of casting by moving the rod with your wrist, which can be a nasty habit to shed. My advice is that you aim to keep a firmly locked wrist during practice and allow the arm to deliver the energy to the rod.

Once your motor coordination is consistent, you can soften up a bit and use the wrist constructively in a number of situations.

The wrist fine-tunes the loop

Loading the rod with your wrist is a logical choice when you find yourself wanting to present a fly to a fish that's close by. The goal in a short cast is to present the fly without scaring the fish with large movements. In this situation, you will be able to load the rod with sufficient energy by using your wrist as a primary source.

The wrist is also used to fine-tune the speed of the loop in the forward cast. If you realize that the speed of the loop is too high and the leader is about to punch down hard on the surface, you can bend the wrist forward and lower the rod. This change will increase the speed on the lower line and make the rotation speed of the wheel drop.

On the other hand, if the speed of the loop is too low and the upper line contains too little energy to stretch out properly in the forward cast, do the opposite. Turn the wrist upward and the rod will be lifted, which will give you a larger resistance on the lower line and increase the speed on the upper line, making the leader stretch out.

Finally, you can add extra power toward the final phase of the forward cast by using the lower arm and wrist. When the upper arm has completed its share of the energy transfer, the rod can be led forward— by stretching out the lower arm and tipping the wrist downward a bit—to finish the cast. Do not lower the rod tip too much: in a long cast it is important to aim a little high in the forward cast to ensure a long descent of the line; otherwise, it will be hard to send the line flying over long distances.

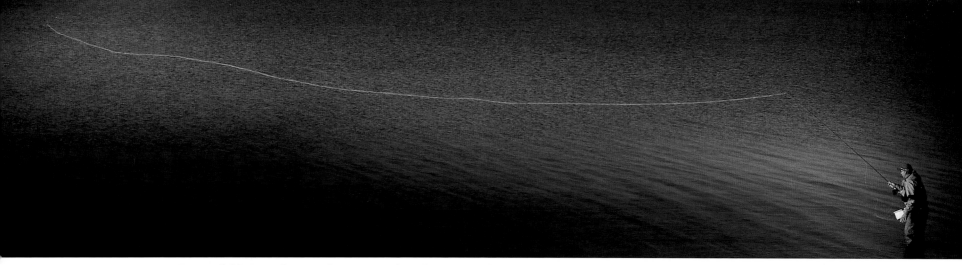

Figure 4-18. You often need to cover a lot of water on the seashore, and this is where the long overhead cast comes into play. Langeland, Denmark.

Long overhead casts with a single-handed rod

I have to admit that I hesitated a bit before writing this section. Attention in the last few years has increasingly focused on impressive casting distances, which are in my opinion above and beyond the needs of a fly fisherman. A long fly cast does not necessarily equal a good cast for fishing. Short, accurate, and controlled casting is often superior to a long line, particularly in running water. But while I'm not normally in favor of long casting, certain situations do require a long cast. Shore fishing, where you need to send long and powerful casts in a gale force wind, across reefs and forests of seaweed, in pursuit of fast-swimming saltwater species, is an example.

Even though precision is not always critical, you will feel a sense of accomplishment when you send a long line flying and see the leader stretch out nicely.

> **A long cast takes technical skills**
> Given a perfect technique, the only limitation of line acceleration is raw power. To most casters, however, the limiting factor is not strength but technique. Stay with the double-haul practice for long casting (refer to chapter 6) until you've got it right. The rod movements during the cast also need to be fully controlled so that the rod is led straight back and forth in the same plane, not circling around. If the rod is doing a circle arc, the loss of energy is considerable and will result in a shorter cast.

Longer casting with a long belly

You saw in chapter 3 that a long and heavy belly, in most situations, is not an advantage. But if your goal is long casting, using a long belly may be an advantage. A belly is usually around 10–11 meters, but if you use one of 11–12 meters, it will take longer to roll out completely, meaning that the potential for a longer cast is definitely there.

The longer belly must fit the rod: it cannot be heavier than a normal belly.

The precondition for a long cast is a deeper drift. The idea is that the stretch between the back position and the front is extended. But in order to cash in on the extra effort this takes, you have to maintain a straight casting plane without a circular motion.

Take one step back

In order to do a deeper drift without circling, take one step back so your right leg (if you're a right-handed caster) is behind your left leg. Standing like this, you'll be able to pull your right arm farther back and achieve a deeper drift.

Figure 4-19. The drift gets deeper if you step back on your right foot.

In review, to get a long stretch for acceleration during a long cast, do a deeper drift to move the back position farther back. The last onset of force comes from moving the lower

Figure 4-20. The deep drift allows the rod to accelerate over a longer stretch.

arm forward in the forward cast and using the wrist to finish off the cast.

Unfortunately, all these changes lead to a low front stop. You might think that a lower front stop would lead to a larger loop, but that is something we particularly want to avoid in a long cast because of a greater wind resistance and the cast being easily caught by crosswinds.

Figure 4-20 illustrates the principle behind a long cast. The deep drift leads to a back position that is below the front stop. Yet the loop is narrow because the size of the loop is determined by the height difference between the front stop and the back position.

A lower front stop loads the blank more to make it work deeper and store more energy. Energy will then send the loop flying with a very high initial speed.

In a longer cast, the angle of the cast is larger than normal. But don't overdo it; the result may be that the line will hang dangerously low in the backcast. And because of the long length of line, it will take a long time to descend, perhaps ending up in the unpleasant company of bushes, rocks, or other natural elements behind the caster.

A long cast takes a long leader

To cast optimally, you have to get the tackle right—first and foremost, the leader. The role of the leader in the fly cast is balancing the resistance from the lower line. Ideally, the upper line should have just a little more speed than the lower line. This arrangement causes a loop to form for a longer period of time, and as long as you have a loop and a wheel rolling forward, the loop will pull out running line toward the horizon. When the loop rolls out and the line is stretched in the forward cast, you cease to shoot line and the line just descends toward the water. Typically you need a longer leader than normal for long casts. When you add the extra length, the wheel in the loop will turn as slowly as possible, while both the upper and lower line maintain a high momentum.

Figure 4-21 shows how a longer leader decreases the rotation speed and keeps the loop going longer. When you want to do longer casting, use a leader and fly with a mass as close to that of the lower line as possible. Keep the mass of

the lower line greater; otherwise, line and leader will never stretch out toward the end of the cast.

The arrows in the illustration depict the speed of the upper line, lower line, and loop with a long and short leader, respectively.

In the top drawing, the relationship between the masses is wrong: the mass of the upper line is too small. This means that the upper line will have considerably more speed than the lower line, and since the difference of speed between the upper and lower line equals the rotational speed of the loop, this cast will stretch fast and descend without shooting any line worth mentioning.

In the lower drawing, the masses are balanced correctly: the upper line is given a little more speed than the lower line. This balance will turn the wheel slowly. The tackle is optimally adjusted for a long cast.

The fine-tuning between the lower and upper line is done by harmonizing the leader and fly so their mass is in correct proportion to the lower line. A big fly takes a shorter leader; extend the leader when you change to a smaller fly.

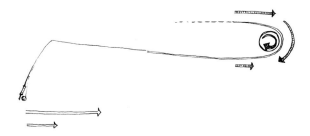

A short leader will give you a high rotational speed = short casting.

Figure 4-21. A long leader will decrease the speed of the wheel and you will be able to shoot a longer line.

Chapter 5

The Scandinavian Spey Cast with a Single-Handed Rod

A huge, well-hooked sea trout caught on a sinking line in the River Menendez, Argentina.

The only necessary cast…

The Scandinavian Spey cast is the only cast you will need for fly fishing in running water where you have the opportunity to walk along the water's edge. You can do this cast even if you can't do a regular overhead cast due to obstacles like bushes, rocks, or trees along the bank. With a Spey cast, you can now cover water previously inaccessible: all of a sudden, you can move from looking for water you *can* fish to searching for places you would *prefer* to fish.

Another asset of the Spey cast is that it requires no false casting, which may spook the fish. And because the fly is never behind you, the risk of hooking yourself or someone else with a wayward fly is reduced dramatically.

Finally, you can fish with the comforting assurance that you have a whole fly at the end of the leader. Every year lots of fish are lost because they took a fly that came into close contact with rocks in the backcast and broke a point. Both salmon and sea trout are hard enough to catch as it is; there is no sensible reason why you should put yourself through the possibility of losing a fish due to a damaged fly.

The Scandinavian Spey cast can be varied to cope with almost any scenario: from long casting with monofilament leaders to extremely angled casting with fast sinking lines. You can also do a parachute cast, a serpentine cast, a snake cast, a pile cast, and other specialized casts that have their basis in the Spey cast. With a curve cast, you can make the leader land in an up- or downstream curve.

You also work your way up from the basic cast in the Scandinavian Spey cast. As with the overhead cast, you need to master this cast to perfection before you can start practicing the many variations that you will need during practical fishing.

The cast from the River Spey

Only a few similarities exist between the Scandinavian Spey cast and the classic Spey cast, which was originally developed along the great Scottish salmon rivers such as the River Spey, which lent its name to this popular cast. The obvious common point of reference between the two is that the line is not lifted behind the caster. Instead the rod is loaded by a large D-shaped loop, which is anchored on the water beside the caster. The main difference is that the classic Spey cast is done with a whole, preferably double-taper fly line. which is attached to the water.

In a classic Spey cast, it is the grip of the surface tension that allows you to form the loop you need to send fly line, leader, and fly back across the stream.

It doesn't get more exhilarating than this: the fly has fished its way across the current, and when the angler strips the line, the salmon follows the fly—the shadow to the far left. Miðfjarðará, Iceland.

In the Scandinavian Spey cast, the loose bellies or shooting heads attached to a running line are used. Of course, you can also use a weight-forward line. Only the leader is used as an anchor on the surface. This difference gives the Scandinavian Spey cast an inherent advantage when it comes to distribution of energy during the cast. You can angle the cast sharply and cast under extremely tight conditions.

In the classic Spey cast, you work with a virtually fixed length of line and you do not shoot much line during casting. As a result, the D-shaped loop behind the caster is rather large, and as a rule, the angler is forced to wade out into the stream to get enough room for the loop.

There are a number of differences between the traditional Spey cast and the modern Scandinavian version of the Spey cast, and both have inherent advantages and drawbacks. I am personally convinced that the Scandinavian Spey cast is a more flexible cast and can be varied to suit most fishing conditions. When the term Spey cast comes up from now on in this book, it refers to the above-mentioned Scandinavian Spey cast.

The roll cast

The roll cast is another version where the friction between leader and water is used as an anchor for the fly line. The roll cast differs from the various types of Spey casts in that you drag line and leader across the surface to the firing position and let the line hang from the tip guide before the line is cast back out. In the Spey cast, the fly line actually leaves the water momentarily, until the leader lands near the caster and anchors the line before it is sent back across the stream in a loop.

Even though it is possible to roll cast a certain amount of line, and also to angle the cast to a certain degree, I will not explain the roll cast further because it gives you no advantage over the Scandinavian Spey cast. Many fly fishermen, however, use the roll cast as a part of the lift, especially when casting with fast sinking lines. These lines are so heavy and hang so deep in the water that you cannot pull them straight out of the water in the lift. Instead, the fly line is rolled to the surface with a roll cast and then cast from that point with an overhead or Spey cast.

This technique gives you one major disadvantage: you can easily disturb the water and force fish from their lies along your own bank. Even if you roll the line close to your own bank, it makes so much splashing and disturbance that sooner or later a fish near your bank will be spooked, destroying your chances of covering unsuspecting fish in front of you.

In chapter 8, you can read about a much more elegant way to pull out a fast sinking line and lay it up for a new cast.

The principle behind the Scandinavian Spey cast

The Scandinavian Spey cast is a great cast to work and pretty to watch. One of the fascinating things about this cast is the dynamics of the loop. It appears almost magical when the line is sent flying high above the water in a perfect loop in the forward cast. In order to become a good Spey caster and perform the cast easily and elegantly, you must understand the principles that make this cast possible.

Figure 5-1 captures the stage in the Spey cast where the forward cast is initiated. The rod is curved slightly back, indicating that the forward motion has started. The loop is in the process of closing, but the leader is still clinging to the surface. In the photo, the rod tip and the back point of the loop are marked with crosses. The part of the line between the crosses is called the active line because this part is set in motion in the forward cast. The connection between the fly line and leader is marked with a circle. The line between the circle and the rear X is the passive part of the line.

In this situation, the leader is anchored to the water's surface beside the caster, meaning that the active line and the passive line are more or less equal in length. If the caster had been standing in a spot with less room behind him, he would

Figure 5-1. The active line is seen between the crosses. The longer this part is, the more energy you'll have at your disposal to pull out the passive line—the line between the cross at the back and the circle.

have to attach the leader farther downstream. If the point of anchorage is in front of the caster, the active line is shorter than the passive line. If enough room is available, the leader can be anchored well behind the caster, making the active line considerably longer than the passive line.

When you move the point of attachment forward with a fixed length of line, you have a shorter active line to set in motion and the passive line is correspondingly longer. The ratio of length between the active and the passive line is determined from the position of the leader in the backcast. With practice, you will be able to control this ratio so the active part is as long as possible, while you keep it clear of branches, bank-side vegetation, rocks, and other obstacles.

You might think that the shorter active line you can cast, the less room you'll need to maneuver so casting will be easier. But casting with a short active line takes quite a bit of skill on the part of the caster, including more accurate timing in the forward cast and a more powerful acceleration of the rod. The rod must be loaded with a shorter line, which means that you have to put more energy into the rod in the forward movement.

Figure 5-2. The force exerted by the surface tension on the leader is termed a "constraint."

In figure 5-2, the loop is rolling forward after the rod is stopped in the front stop. The leader is still attached to the surface because the grip of the surface tension is greater than the pull from the loop rolling forward. The leader will cling to the surface until the pull from the upper line exceeds the force of the surface tension. This force is called the constraint. The design of the leader is one factor that decides the amount of constraint.

The balance in Spey casting tackle

Balance among rod, line, and leader is a precondition for all fly casting, but the threshold of tolerance is lower for the Scandinavian Spey cast than for other types of casting. You can do a relatively good overhead cast even if your tackle was put together a bit haphazardly. But if the tackle is not put together exactly right, it is practically impossible to do a Spey cast!

The leader must be correctly adjusted if you want to Spey cast. If you fish with a leader that is too long, the surface tension on the leader is too high and the constraint on it is too strong. In such a situation, the leader will never let go of the water. If the leader is too short, the force exerted by the surface tension on the leader is too small and the constraint too

weak. In this case, the leader will loose its grip on the water too soon, and there is a risk that it will bounce back behind you and end up in bank-side trees or bushes.

In figure 5-2, no line is shot out, so the lower line of the loop is fixed. Because the upper line moves forward at the same time, the wheel will also roll forward. This same principle is seen in the overhead cast, where the rotational speed of the wheel equals the difference in speed between the lower line and the upper line.

You can also study the Scandinavian Spey cast by looking at the loop. Look at figures 5-1 and 5-2 and notice how every curve in the cast is harmonious and unbroken. This cast is a joy to look at, but it also points out that the casting style is close to ideal. Elimination of line slack throughout the cast, combined with precise stops, is a precondition for efficient casts and leads to low energy consumption.

The casting weight

The chance of throwing a decent Spey cast is determined, among other things, by how long and heavy the casting part of the line is. And as described in chapter 3, the length of the casting belly is the critical factor in Spey casting. In the following section, I will elaborate on the problems arising if the casting belly is either too short or too long.

Figure 5-3. The D-shaped loop sends the line forward in an angle close to horizontal.

Figure 5-3 depicts a Spey cast with a correct length of line. The rod is drawn in two different stages of the cast: just before the forward cast is initiated and just before the leader lifts from the surface at the end of the forward cast (the farther movement of the line is depicted to the far right). Two factors combine to make the cast point straight ahead. First, the front part of the active line is close to horizontal, meaning that the line is already headed in the direction it is going to be sent. Second, the leader does not slip from the surface too soon.

Figure 5-4. Short casting belly: the leader loses its grip too soon.

Figure 5-4 shows a corresponding Spey cast, but in this situation, the casting belly is too short. If the leader is anchored to the water at the same place, the active part of the line will be shorter, which means that less energy will go into the cast. You can compensate for this loss to a certain degree by increasing speed in the forward cast, but this will make the cast more difficult to control. Another problem with Spey casting a short belly is that the front part of the active line is not close to horizontal. In addition, the leader loses its grip on the surface much too soon. Combine these factors and the direction of the cast will be angled upward.

Figure 5-5. A long casting belly takes up more space.

Figure 5-5 shows a cast where the belly is too long. The appearance of this cast resembles the one in figure 5-3, where the cast is performed with a correct length of line. The difference is that the D-shaped loop behind the caster becomes much deeper. In this situation, the benefits of the Spey cast disappear because you have to wade farther out from the bank to get enough room for the line behind you.

The more line you have outside the tip guide, the more room you need behind you. And for this reason, a long belly is a bad choice.

> **The discreet Spey cast**
> As I see it, the big advantage with the Spey cast is that you can perform it standing on the bank between trees or with rocks and bushes behind you, while still being able to cast your line and present the fly. This means that you can cover more holding spots and fish in a more discreet manner.

The leader
The design of the leader decides how much anchor effect you get when the leader is attached to the surface. Length and tapering need to be measured out carefully, and a monofilament leader should be considerably longer than an intermediate polyleader. In practice, the monofilament leader often has to be between one quarter to one half of a rod length longer than the polyleader in order to maintain the same surface tension and grip. (For more information, turn to the tables showing differences in lengths on pages 69 and 71.)

If the leader is too short, it will attach poorly in the backcast. Figure 5-6 shows a situation where the leader touches the surface too late and slides backward, resulting in a solid hookup in a branch of the tree.

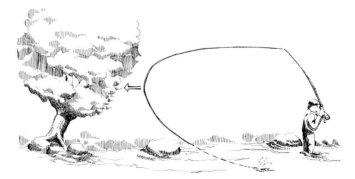

Figure 5-6. Short leader = poor anchor effect on the surface.

Differences between overhead casting and Spey casting
The Scandinavian Spey cast is often compared to the overhead cast, and some claim that the movements of the two are similar. That claim is incorrect. Apart from the simple fact that the line is lifted below the rod instead of over the rod, several crucial differences exist between the overhead and Spey cast. One major difference is that the entire movement backward in the overhead cast is done in one plane: If you look at the

fly caster from above, the line forms a linear movement backward and forward. In the Scandinavian Spey cast only the lift is linear; the rest of the backward movement is a semicircle.

The lift

In the Scandinavian Spey cast, the lift is done with a slow but steady rise to the front stop. The goal is to lift the line clear of the water while the leader is still anchored to the surface. Next, the line in the backcast can be led from the front stop to the firing position with an increased acceleration, which makes the line swing below the rod and allows the leader to land on the water next to the caster.

Figure 5-7. In the backcast, the line flies backward until the leader is anchored next to the angler.

The lift and front stop are the same in Spey casting and overhead casting. Make sure that the lift is done with a steady rise of the rod in one plane without angling the rod outward. Seen from above, the line should be a direct extension of the rod when the rod is in the front stop. Seen from the side, the leader should just cling to the surface when the rod is in the front stop. At this point the next acceleration starts. (See figure 5-7.)

The backcast

From the front stop, you move to the last and final acceleration in the backward movement. Here you will experience the main difference between Spey casting and overhead casting. In the overhead cast, the movement from the front stop to the firing position is split around the rear stop where the rod is stopped and passes over to an even movement during the drift. The rod passes directly from the front stop to the firing position in the Scandinavian Spey cast, as shown in figure 5-8. The speed is increased from the front stop to the firing position in order to lift the leader clear of the water and move both the line and leader backward.

If you want the leader to touch the surface evenly, the rod must not dive at any point during the movement backward.

In practice, the rod moves in an ever-increasing curve during the entire movement from the front stop to the firing position. Just before you reach the firing position, the tip guide describes a steep angle upward in a final lift.

Figure 5-8. The backcast is the movement from the front stop to the firing position.

Seen from above, the rod tip should move in a flat semicircle. The best way to achieve this is by rotating your lower arm outward while your elbow is slightly closed and lifted, as seen in figure 5-9. The evenly rising tip guide is described more in the following section about anchoring the leader on the surface.

Figure 5-9. Spey casting with a single-handed rod: the rod is led in a small semicircle backward and outward before it is moved to a vertical position, allowing you to lead it forward in the vertical plane in the forward cast.

A calm casting style will result in calm and composed loops. In short, do not use more muscle than needed; let the rod do the work for you.

As stated before, the tip guide should make a semicircular movement. This semicircle must be as flat as possible so the leader can anchor itself to the water surface close to the caster. The larger the semicircle is, the farther away from the caster the leader will land.

In a longer cast, the firing position will be farther back and a rotation of the arm will not do the job on its own. You will also have to rotate the torso and hip as well.

Make sure that the rotation of the torso is initiated only after the rod has been momentarily checked in the front stop, another precondition for keeping the leader close to the body.

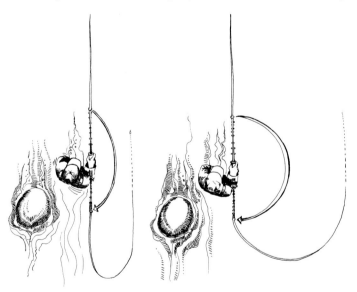

Figure 5-10. The movements of the rod during a Spey cast, as seen from above. The flatter you can make the semicircular movement, the closer to you the leader will land.

The movement of the rod in a semicircle is shown in figure 5-10. Notice that the leader to the left is anchored close to the caster and almost completely straight. The bigger the semicircle you make, the less power you have stored for the forward cast, because you have to pick up the line from your side (see the illustration to the right).

Anchoring the leader on the surface

In practice, the fly will often be the first object to make contact with the surface, followed by the leader and starting with the leader tip.

Problems arise, however, if the middle or butt section of the leader is the first part to touch the surface. The backward movement of the leader is instantaneously stopped the moment it hits the water, but if the middle section is stopped first, the tip section of the leader will still be traveling backward and thus land in a heap on top of the middle section of the leader. You then have a serious risk of knots, called "wind knots," forming on the leader and the anchoring will be far from even.

If the tip of the actual fly line is the first part to touch the surface, the whole leader will follow it and land in a heap. In such a situation, not only is the leader anchored down, but a part of the line is too. The solid anchor-effect will most likely result in a poorly stretched line in the forward cast. If the line and leader are successfully forced from the surface tension, you will most likely see the line flying in a very unsteady loop.

Even anchoring is achieved by leading the tip guide in a gently rising curve during the movement from the front stop to the firing position (see the top drawing in figure 5-11).

The rod is moved in a gently rising curve, resulting in an even anchoring of the leader.

The ideal D-shaped loop.

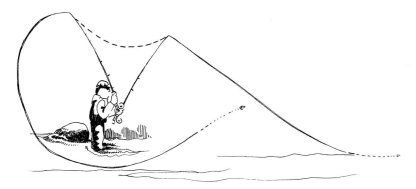

Figure 5-11. If the tip guide dives, the fly line and not the leader will adhere to the surface.

Figure 5-12. A smaller part of the active line is close to horizontal in a circular loop.

The shape of the loop

For better casting, the loop above the anchored leader should be shaped like a D immediately before the forward cast, not a circular loop as once was commonly suggested. The top drawing of figure 5-12 shows the desired D-shaped loop; below it is the more circular version. You could argue that the active part of the line is bigger on the circular loop, but when you compare it to the D-shaped loop, you can see that on the latter a larger part of the line is closer to horizontal. This positioning means that the pull on the loop is more efficient when the rest of the line is being shot the same way—that is, horizontally through the air in front of the caster. Your goal is to have as much of the line as possible in a straight line from the tip guide and backward.

The desired D shape is made by starting the forward cast immediately after the leader has touched the surface. Look

at the top drawing of figure 5-12. You can almost sense how the upper loop could have looked like the one on the lower drawing if the forward cast had not started immediately.

The added bonus of starting the forward cast at the stage where the active line hangs directly back from the tip guide is that you achieve the correct direction in the forward cast: remember, the direction of the line in the backcast decides the direction of the forward cast. If the line is straight back from the tip guide, it will also be traveling straight ahead in the forward cast: the backcast and forward cast are in a straight line. The circular loop, on the other hand, will send the cast flying to the skies, just like a short shooting head does. (See figure 5-4, page 100.)

The forward cast

While there are major differences between the backcast of the Spey cast and the overhead cast, there are none in the forward cast. The forward cast of the Scandinavian Spey cast is identical to the forward cast stages of the overhead cast. When the rod is in the firing position, the elbow is closed and lifted, and the cast is made by pulling the elbow in place. The elbow opens and the lower arm is brought to an almost horizontal position. When the loop is almost unfolded, the rod is gradually lowered, following the movement of the line while it descends.

In order to achieve a narrow loop in the forward cast, aim for as little difference in height as possible between the firing position and the front stop, seen in the direction of the cast. In practice, this means that the rod is stopped at an early stage. The high front stop is shown in figure 5-13.

Figure 5-13. A high front stop will give you a narrow loop.

The angle on the rod

A frequent mistake in the Scandinavian Spey forward cast is moving the rod in a slanting angle outward from the caster, instead of moving it in a vertical plane. The problem is that the loop will have the same angle outward, which causes it to lose energy and prevents the stretch in the line and leader. The line might stretch, however, if you give it a bit of muscle, but this will almost always result in a line that curves left (if you cast with your right hand).

We will return to the problem of the slanting loops in chapter 7 (page 135) in connection with double-handed casting, where the same problem arises if you do not raise the rod to vertical before moving it to the front stop.

To avoid slanting loops, raise the rod to a vertical position before the forward cast is initiated. This movement ensures that the rod is passed forward in the vertical plane, sending the line flying as in the forward cast.

Take another look at figure 5-10, which shows the caster from above. Seen from a bird's-eye perspective, the rod makes a flat semicircle in the Scandinavian Spey cast. The D is drawn by a semicircular movement backward in the backcast and a movement straight ahead in the forward cast.

The complete Spey cast

The series of photos on the next pages shows the Scandinavian Spey cast in its entirety. In figure 5-14, the cast is initiated. The lift sets the line in motion, but the leader is still attached to the surface. The line should have no slack.

Figure 5-14. The lift to the front stop.

In figure 5-15, the rod is in the firing position and still leaning out at an angle from the angler. The leader has lost its grip on the water and flies backward with the line. The line has started to form a D-shaped loop backward. Notice that the line is curving upward and that the tip part is parallel to the water, because the rod tip is describing a rising movement throughout the entire backcast.

Figure 5-15. The firing position.

In figure 5-16, just the leader has touched the water and is anchored there. The rod has returned to the vertical and has left the firing position. The forward cast has started.

Figure 5-16. The forward cast is started the moment the leader is attached to the surface.

In figure 5-17, the forward cast is completed. The rod has been passed forward and is loaded against the active line. The rod has reached the front stop, but the leader is still attached

to the surface. The line is moving forward, and the loop in front of the tip guide is in its earliest stage.

Figure 5-17. The rod is in the front stop—the forward cast is completed.

In figure 5-18, the rod is still in the front stop, but the loop has rolled out to the point where only the very tip of the leader is still on the water.

Figure 5-18. The line rolls out perfectly across the stream.

From now on the loop will keep on rolling. The active part of the line has set the passive part in motion. When the loop is almost unfolded, the caster must prepare to lower the rod gradually, as the line descends towards the water.

Practicing the Spey cast

You will benefit the most from your hours of practicing the Scandinavian Spey cast if you use a floating line and a monofilament leader. Ideally, you should practice at a stream where you can wade out a bit to avoid reeds, bushes, branches, and rocks along the bank. The current will help you stretch out the line even before you start the lift. Do not wade out to your thighs, because the lift will be harder to perform correctly and because the D-shape of the line easily becomes elongated. If you stand in water up to your ankles, you will have full control in your cast.

Even if you don't have a stream nearby, you can still practice the Scandinavian Spey cast. However, it should still be practiced on water. If you can Spey cast in still water, you will be able to Spey cast in running water. And if you get used to the feeling of the current stretching out the leader for you, practicing on the bank of a lake will still be valuable because you may end up having trouble in a slow-moving part of the river if you get too lazy. Start with a line long enough to get a decent angle on the backcast. You'll need about 24 feet of fly line plus a leader of about 12 feet. Notice the following elements in the cast:

- *The lift is made in a straight line followed by a short pause.*
- *The backcast is done by bending the elbow while it is lifted outward, making the tip guide trace a small semicircle.*
- *The tip guide must follow a gradually increasing curve.*
- *The forward cast must be carried out in the vertical plane.*

These points must be followed to do a Spey cast. You can improve your style by trying to place the leader on the water's surface as close to your body as possible. The closer it is to your body, the more energy can you put into the cast.

You can also practice by placing the connection between the line and leader in front of, next to, or behind you. These elements should all be practiced thoroughly before moving on with the Scandinavian Spey cast in actual fishing.

The next step, as in the overhead cast, is how to cast a longer line.

Chapter 6 presents the Scandinavian Spey cast with a single haul, which will add length to your casting. The Scandinavian Spey cast will enable you to angle your cast aggressively (change casting direction), depending on how the line is lifted. When these things are combined, it is surprising how few holding areas you will *not* be able to cover with a fly.

Ideal water for the Scandinavian Spey cast. Miðfjarðará, Iceland.

Chapter 6
Single Haul and Double Haul

A huge sea trout benefitting from catch and release. River Menendez, Argentina.

Pulling the line increases precision

All fly casting is made more efficient when you use a single or double haul. With this pull, you can achieve a stretched line at all times, eliminating any slack line. At the same time, the rod is flexed more when you pull the line, generating more energy in the cast.

I clearly remember the first time I tried to grasp the principles of the double haul by pulling the line in the front and backcast. In the book on fly casting that I studied, the technique was described as the simplest thing in the world. But I will not easily forget the agonizing hardship that followed. When I got it right for the first time and the line simply shot across the water, I had goose bumps up and down my spine.

Hauling when the fish is close

The single and double hauls are surprisingly versatile and are not used just for long-distance casting. The technique also comes in handy for short-distance casting, because you can achieve the same line speed with smaller movements of the rod. This is ideal for fishing close distances because you can send the line flying discreetly: your movements are cut down to a minimum, and the risk of spooking the fish is reduced.

Single and double hauling

Single and double hauls are the most efficient ways to gain precision in all kinds of single-handed casting. Once you master the different basic casts, practice the technique thoroughly. The double haul is used for overhead casting, while the single haul is utilized during Scandinavian Spey casting. After you master the technique, the single and double hauls will become second nature and you will use them in all kinds of situations. The pull will ensure that the rod is steady in the cast and that the cast has a high degree of precision.

Coordinating the casting movements

A pull of the line during either the front or the backcast, or both, is the key. But the pull should be carried out at the right time to gain maximum effect. Earlier, you saw how the forward cast in both the overhead and Spey casts consists of a smooth acceleration from the firing position, ending in a sudden stop in the front stop. The single and double hauls follow this movement: they start slowly, increase in speed, and accelerate before the pull suddenly stops.

The pull counteracts slack line

The pull works in two ways. First, in the initial phase, where the speed of the line is not yet very high, the pull acts to ensure a completely stretched line and a correct placement of the line in relation to the forward cast and backcast, before the acceleration properly generates speed to the line. A stretched line without slack is easier to accelerate in the forward cast. If, for some reason, you cannot stretch the line properly in the backcast, the reason could be a strong wind at your back. The pull will reduce that slack.

The pull's main function in the backcast is to help you place the line correctly: when you transfer energy with the hand holding the line, you can pass the rod backward in a slower pace, allowing you to find the firing position with precision. Using the pull will give you more control over the placement of the line in the backcast.

Second, in the last phase of the pull when the speed is highest, the pull will work to increase the energy transfer to the blank, helping you to load more energy. The line will speed up, because a deeply loaded blank will regain a neutral position even more quickly.

Synchronize the pull with the casting hand

Start the pull by placing the hand holding the line (the line hand) close to the rod hand. The pull is done in the same fashion as the movement of the rod: a smooth acceleration followed by a distinct stop, after which the line hand returns to the position close to the rod hand. The line hand is now ready for the next pull.

It is important that the line, as well as the guides on the rod, be kept clean to prevent slack between the stripping guide and the line hand when the latter is passed back to the rod hand. The line will retain its ability to glide smoothly if it is cleaned with a piece of cloth treated with line conditioner after every third or fourth trip. After you have cleaned the line, use the cloth to clean the guides on your rod.

Timing in the pull

Timing is important. The pull generally follows the rod arm, meaning that it starts and stops simultaneously with the casting movements of the casting arm. In the forward cast of the overhead cast and the Spey cast alike, the pull starts when the rod is set in motion from the firing position; it ends at the precise moment the rod is in the front stop.

In the overhead cast, however, the double haul starts the moment the rod passes the front stop; it ends when the rod is in the firing position.

The length of the pull is adjusted to the length of the line being cast, exactly like the casting movement. For short-distance casting, the pull may be no more than 8–16 inches, while for longer casts, it may measure 3 feet.

Figure 6-1 shows you how the backcast pull is done in a movement going *straight down*, while the pull for the forward cast is pulled out *sideways*.

In the forward cast, the pull will increase line speed, which increases the length of the cast. You will need a longer pull in the forward cast, and that can be achieved by pulling the line sideways.

Figure 6-1. The line is pulled straight down in the backcast.

The line is pulled sideways in the forward cast to achieve a longer pull.

Notice in the photo above that the fly line, or running line, is inside the line hand. When you pull hard on the line, lock it down as shown in the close-up photo below. This action will ensure a secure grip on the line, which will come in handy on cold and wet days at the water when the line has a tendency to slip between your fingers and then collapse completely.

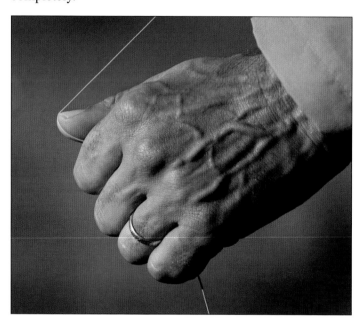

Lock the running line to prevent it from slipping in a critical moment.

When a really long cast is needed, shoot a bit of line in the backcast before the final forward cast. This technique will give the rod a slightly heavier weight to work with, which results in a deeper load of the blank. Another and maybe even more important effect is that you will have a longer upper line, which will keep the wheel rotating longer and subsequently increase the casting length. This benefit only applies if you do not shoot out too much line in the backcast; if you don't, you can cast a very long way with this neat little trick. The initial part of the pull will also help you to stretch the line completely and correctly place the line before the final acceleration.

Overhand casting with double haul

The next series of photos shows how to do the overhead cast with a double haul. The cast starts as a normal overhead cast, but in the front stop, the line hand should more or less follow the rod hand, as shown in figure 6-2.

Figure 6-2. The line hand is placed close to the rod hand during the lift.

In figure 6-3, the rod is very close to the front stop and the rod and line hands are still close to each other. When the rod has passed the front stop, the speed on the rod arm is increased while the pull on the line begins.

Figure 6-3. The rod is close to the front stop.

When the rod has passed the front stop, the backcast is made with an accelerating movement of both the casting arm and the line hand. In figure 6-4, the rod is in the firing position—no loop has been formed yet—and the line hand has also reached its outermost position. As you can see, the pull for the backcast is not particularly long—in this case, maybe around 1 ½ feet.

Figure 6-4. The pull is synchronized with the movement of the casting arm.

In figure 6-5, the drift is made. The rod is on its way to the firing position and a loop has been formed; the line hand has been pulled down a bit farther and the pull stops in this position. After this step, the hand is passed back to a position close to the rod hand, at a pace slow enough to prevent slack between the line hand and the stripping guide.

Figure 6-5. After the drift, the line hand is passed back to the rod hand.

A good conclusion to a perfect cast: the sea trout is bulging beneath the dry fly. Rock Splash Pool, Rio Grande, Argentina.

In Figure 6-6, the rod is still in the firing position and the line is almost stretched out in the backcast. The line hand is now back with the rod hand, ready to pull the line for the forward cast, which is about to start.

The forward cast is on its way in figure 6-7, and the rod is almost in the front stop. No loop has formed yet because the rod is only just about to be stopped. The line hand is down and sideways in a forceful pull, which is now almost complete.

Figure 6-6. The forward cast can begin and the line hand is ready for a new pull.

Figure 6-7. During the forward cast, the line is pulled down and sideways in order to achieve the longest possible pull.

Figure 6-8. The rod is in the front stop and the line hand in its outmost position.

In figure 6-8, the rod is brought to a complete halt in the front stop and a fine loop is formed. The line hand is in its outermost position, where it stops completely. If you want to shoot line at this stage, loosen your firm grip on the running line. Don't let go of the line altogether, but merely let it run through an O-shaped grip formed by your thumb and index finger. This change lets you maintain control of the line and ensures that you are ready to fish the moment the fly lands on the surface.

Notice the perfectly elliptical loop shooting across the water. Such a cast can go a long way because it has a long time to descend and because the compact shape of the loop creates little resistance during its flight.

Notice also how the upper line has descended to the point where it crosses the lower line. This situation is frequently seen in a longer cast, where it is necessary to work with a wider angle on the cast. Even though this arrangement seems like it should give you problems—such as the leader snagging on the line—they rarely happen in practice.

Scandinavian Spey casting with single haul

The Scandinavian Spey cast is, in itself, a very efficient cast. However, if you add the single haul to the forward cast, you will be well prepared to tackle streams with plenty of bank-side vegetation, rocks, and other challenges along the water's edge. You will also be well equipped to tackle demanding situations requiring a longer cast. The single haul is, in fact, the only way you can supply energy and length, and still be in control of both loop and direction of the cast.

Figure 6-9. Ready for Spey casting with a single haul.

Figure 6-9 shows the starting position; the previous cast is fished through. The rod is pointing in the direction of the line and the loose line is collected in loops, with the first and largest one held by the pinkie finger, while the ring finger holds a second and slightly smaller loop.

In Figure 6-10, the cast is halfway through the lift phase and the line hand is on its way to a position close to the casting hand.

In the photo of Figure 6-11, the lift is carried out and the rod is in the front stop. The leader is still attached to the surface, making the line form a straight line from the tip guide to the surface. The line hand is in place next to the rod hand.

Figure 6-10. When the lift is made, the line hand and the rod hand should be close to each other.

Figure 6-11. The rod hand will bring the rod back to the firing position from the front stop.

Figure 6-12: Seen from above, the rod should describe a flat semicircle, which will make the leader land in close proximity to the fly fisher.

The rod is now passed from the front stop through a small semicircle directly to the firing position because the back stop is left out in Spey casting. In Figure 6-12, the rod is in the firing position and the line is traveling backward.

The leader has lost its grip on the surface and, seen from the side, line and leader form a concave curve. The moment the leader lands on the surface, the front cast is initiated and the single haul is performed with the line hand.

Figure 6-13. The leader kisses the surface before the forward cast sends fly line and leader back across the stream.

In Figure 6-14, the leader has just landed on the surface and the front cast has started. Notice the rod bending against the pull of the line and also the line hand on its way sideways. The leader can be seen touching the surface of the water next to the fly fisher.

In Figure 6-14, the forward cast is complete: the rod is in its front stop and the hand in its outmost position. A loop is formed, but the leader is still attached to the surface. The running line is not released yet, but when it is, it will be pulled out by the loop rolling forwards.

Figure 6-14. Notice the fine-looking D-shaped curve behind the caster and the beginning of a handsome and narrow loop in the air in front of the tip guide.

Figure 6-15. The pull with the left hand adds lots of energy to the cast and helps the casting arm in its calm and precise movement forward.

Chapter 7

Casting with a Double-Handed Rod

It is easier to control and maneuver the fly swimming across the current with a long double-handed rod. Rio Grande, Argentina.

Double-handed rods—more popular than ever

Over the years, development of double-handed rods has been pushed forward due to tackle design initiatives from Europe and Scandinavia. These great leaps forward in tackle development give the angler better access to well-balanced and functional tackle, which in turn makes it easier to come to terms with double-handed casting techniques.

Long-standing traditions call for short single-handed rods for salmon fishing in the United States and Canada. These traditions come mainly from the legendary salmon angler and writer Lee Wulff (1905–1991), who started promoting rods as short as 6–7 feet for salmon fishing as early as the 1940s. Wulff caught many large salmon on short single-handed rods with flies as small as size 16.

Compared to the heavy split cane and fiberglass rods, which dominated the market all the way up to the 1970s, these ultrashort fly rods were easier to handle throughout a day's fishing. These rod types were then replaced by carbon fiber, which made its breakthrough in rod building around the early 1980s and soon became the leading star due to its superior strength in relation to weight.

Wulff had another weighty argument for using single-handed rods for salmon: they were more suited for dry-fly fishing because you could handle the loose line with one hand and constantly strip line or release it back accordingly as the dry fly rode the current. This last argument is still valid today. The single-handed rod is the obvious choice for both dry-fly and hitch-fly fishing. For all other disciplines in salmon and sea-trout fishing, the double-handed rod is an appropriate tool to use, and modern double-handed rods actually weigh less than the short single-handed rods used by Wulff.

You cannot underestimate, however, Lee Wulff's impact on generations of anglers picking up their favorite rod for a day of fly fishing. I have spotted American anglers in the distance on numerous occasions, and their short rods are a sure sign of their country of origin.

Today, the tide has turned and fishing with light double-handed rods is the fastest expanding branch of fishing in the United States and Canada.

Ironically, this trend is based on developments rooted in Scandinavia. There, double-handed rods and salmon fishing have been firmly intertwined concepts since the end of the nineteenth century when English lords sailed across the North Sea to explore the riffles of salmon rivers in Norway and Sweden. The Englishmen brought long wooden rods, silk lines, and elaborately designed flies and founded salmon and sea-trout angling.

The rods used at that time were made of greenheart, a tropical tree native to South America. Greenheart wood is hard, heavy, densely structured, and extremely strong—more than twice as strong as oak.

The carbon fiber revolution started in the 1980s, more than 100 years later. Lighter, thinner, stronger, and faster rods appeared on the market, and double-handed rods were no longer just a tool for large salmon rivers. Light rods of 11–13 feet found their way to the smaller rivers and streams of Norway, Sweden, Finland, Denmark, and Iceland.

Just as the single-handed rod is used for a variety of angling situations, the double-handed rod is also a versatile tool, from the smallest rods of 11–12 feet, classified as 5, 6, 7, and 8, to the powerful 15–16 feet rods, class 11 and 12.

A somewhat longer and stronger rod is the ideal choice for fishing the big rivers with a sinking line and big flies. But the shorter double-handed rods have also become favorites in many anglers' armories for fishing sea trout and grilse in small rivers. The extra length of these rods will give you an edge when reeds and bushes obstruct the riverbanks and an advantage when you fight a larger fish.

The double-handed rod for superior fly control

The single most important reason why I prefer the double-handed rod is that a double-handed rod will give me the best possible opportunities to control the course of the fly. This argument should be textbook to all fly fishing, because the way the fly fishes determines if you catch anything at all.

The double-handed rod is superior for mending lines—on a short as well as a long line. When the line is on the water, mending will enable you to park the fly on a given holding spot in the river, and you can also accelerate the fly or make it fish slower.

The long rod enables us to work the line continually and affect how the fly moves in the water. When you work the fly through the line, you will actually get a real sense of being a fly fisher. Simply put, the double-handed rod expands your possibilities more than a single-handed rod could.

Spey, Scandinavian Spey, and Skagit

Several different variations, or schools, exist within double-handed casting. One is the classic Spey cast. It evolved along with double-handed fishing in the classic salmon rivers, like the River Spey in Scotland. Relatively long rods, around 15

Double-handed tackle in action on a fine fall day on the river Mörrum. A beautiful setting where Spey casting comes into its own.

feet, with a parabolic action (full action) are used for Spey casting. The lines themselves are also long, either double-taper or weight-forward lines, with a long casting belly (long belly). Normally, only a short line is shot out in the forward cast during a Spey cast, which means that you do not have to strip in any great length of line before a new cast is initiated.

An alternative casting style involving short but fast rods developed in Scandinavia around the 1980s. Double-taper and weight-forward lines were put aside and the so-called shooting head systems saw the light of day. These 10–14-meter long casting bellies (shooting heads) were connected to a thin, smooth running line, enabling the caster to shoot a great length of line.

One major advantage with this new casting style is that it uses a minimum amount of space allowing you to angle your cast more radically. With this cast, you can cover more potential holding areas and still keep disturbances on the water to a minimum.

Overall, the main benefit of the Spey cast is that it lets you fish close to, or even from the bank when you cover a pool or a neck. You can cover the holding spots from the middle of the river to your own bank in a far more efficient manner. And it will always be easier to control the fly on a short line, with the added benefit that you can spot potential fish reacting to the fly but not necessarily taking.

The traditional Spey fisher has to move out in the river a bit, which will inevitably scare nearby fish. This scenario is not good news for the angler fishing behind the wading Spey caster either.

Double-handed tackle became popular on the major Pacific American and Canadian steelhead rivers in the 1990s. Casting style and tackle composition have found a niche between the Scandinavian and the British here, which typically means that fast 13–14 rods are used in combination with long belly lines. Incidentally, all double-handed rods are termed Spey rods in North America.

The American casting style is often labeled Skagit, after a large river in Washington State, one of the first places where double-handed rods made an entry on the American fly-fishing scene. Steelhead run the Skagit River in the winter, which means that heavy sinking lines and large flies are the accepted norm.

> When the fly line or the leader touches the water in the traditional Spey cast (and in the Scandinavian Spey cast), it is a brief affair; more a gentle kiss than a splash.

In the Skagit casting style, however, the fly line is solidly locked down. The lift resembles the lift of a Spey cast, but the moment the fly and leader touch the water next to the caster, the rod is pushed forward. This stroke of the rod means that the line is laid down twice in front of the angler. The rod is flexed when the doubled line is lifted back from the water to form a D in the backcast, which otherwise is just like a normal Spey cast.

This means that, in fact, we have three different kinds of Spey casting: a traditional British Spey casting style, a Scandinavian style and the North American Skagit style. In this book, I will stick to the style that I know well, the Scandinavian casting style.

Three types of fly casting

You can choose from a wide array of named casts with the double-handed rod, but they can be divided into three main categories:

- *The overhead cast*
- *The roll cast*
- *The Spey cast*

The overhead cast may have been somewhat overlooked in recent years. The tendency has been to consider the use of the different variations of the Spey cast as the "proper" thing to do, where the line can be cast regardless of bank-side vegetation, trees, or other obstacles behind the angler.

Never underestimate the overhead cast

The overhead cast provides a range of possibilities and will out-fish all other casts, provided you have enough space to execute the cast. First, this cast will create much less noise and disturbance on the water, which is a major advantage on quiet and slow flowing parts of the river. Second, it is also more precise because the overhead cast is made higher above the water, which in turn gives the angler more time for corrections while the line is still in the air. And finally, the overhead cast gives the longest cast. A long cast is not always better, but sometimes it may be necessary to reach that far-off holding spot close to the other bank.

The roll cast differs from the Spey cast because the line never leaves the water in the backcast. The roll cast does not offer any major advantages over a Spey cast or overhead cast, but it is useful when fishing fast sinking lines.

The Spey cast is the classic double-handed cast, and in the United States and Canada it is synonymous with double-handed fishing. The British tradition holds two major varieties of the Spey cast: single and double Spey cast.

My version of the single Spey cast is presented in this chapter. Note that a single Spey cast that is not done at an angle is also called a switch cast. The double Spey cast is useful in downstream wind or for casting from the right side of the river with the right hand on top of the rod handle. But these challenges can be handled more efficiently by learning to cast with the left hand on top, rather than using the double Spey. (Read more about that technique in chapter 8.)

The Scandinavian version of single Spey is, not surprisingly, termed the Scandinavian Spey cast. It differs from the traditional Spey cast on several crucial points. I have chosen not to use the Swedish term underhand cast. This is because the cast I practice contains two essential points, which are a partial transmission of power via the upper hand and a rotation of the body. These points differ a great deal from the original description of the underhand cast made by the Swede Göran Andersson. This distinction is not meant as a critique of the underhand cast: Göran is an excellent caster who has inspired many to venture into the world of fly casting, and I hold a profound respect for his efforts, but even if the two casting styles have a common denominator, there are more differences nonetheless.

Choice of line system

For the lighter single-handed rods in classes 3–7, I advocate a whole weight-forward line. The weight-forward line is second to none: excellent cast ability and trouble-free handling. But for the double-handed rod, things look different. In this case, I practically always use a line system with loose bellies (shooting heads).

As described in chapter 3, the shooting head system for double-handed rods is nowhere near the systems used for actual competition casting, where the goal is to cast the farthest possible, which means using (overly) heavy bellies attached to thin running lines. On the contrary, I see more common reference points between a traditional weight-forward line and my line systems, the modified weight forward (MWF) and the personalized weight forward (PWF).

Opponents of line systems incorporating loose bellies are in favor of whole lines, which means double-taper (DT) and weight-forward (WF) lines. Their argument is that by fishing a fixed length of line, you will gain more efficient fishing time, because you do not waste time stripping the line between casts. However, this argument is only valid if you presume that stripping the loose or running line is actually a waste of time. Seen from another perspective, you could also argue that stripping the line is actually a highly efficient way to fish your fly.

When you pull the line back along your own bank (stripping), you are actually covering your own side of the river, a thing that you cannot accomplish as efficiently with a fixed line. This is an irrelevant feature for the guy fishing the double-taper line; he is forced to wade out into the river quite a bit to have the space required to build up the D-shaped loop behind him, and a wading angler will inevitably scare some of the fish standing close to his own bank. A spooked fish is extraordinarily hard to tempt with a small metal hook disguised in a few feathers.

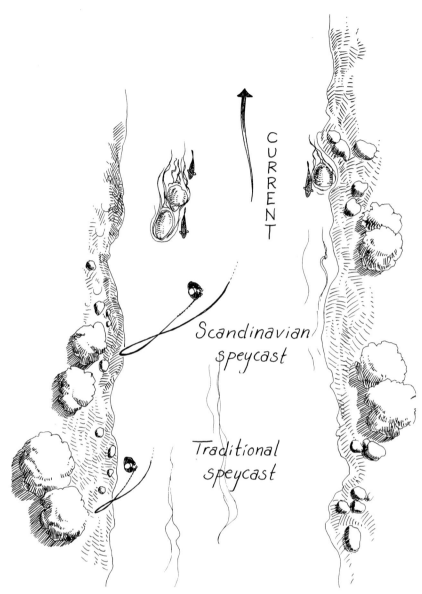

Figure 7-1. The Scandinavian Spey cast is carried out from a position closer to the bank because of the shorter casting belly.

> **Fish the stream—don't wade it!**
> That title may seem like a somewhat hard-and-fast rule, but it's still a piece of good advice that can frequently turn a mediocre day of fly fishing on the stream into a day to remember.

Stripping the fly back is also essential when you need to give the impression of life to the fly while you are fishing a calm section of the river.

You often hear that it is hard to hook a fish when the line is hanging straight downstream. Throughout the years, I have landed quite a few salmon from that exact position. The solid strikes were induced just as the cast had been fished through and the line stripped for a new cast.

For many anglers, the problem is that they have poor contact with the fly when it is just hanging passively at the end of the line swimming downstream parallel to their own bank. Because the take is frequently little more than a delicate tug of the line rather than a regular solid hookup, the angler will often miss the opportunity altogether because the fish is poorly hooked.

When the fly crosses the river and enters calmer waters, I strip the line by hand. If the fly at the end of the leader is a large one, I will strip it relatively fast. The materials on the hook should pulse and the fly should swim with lifelike action, creating the impression of an attractive prey. The current along your own bank is rarely forceful enough to keep a large fly swimming on its own accord; you will need to speed things up a bit.

A smaller fly, on the other hand, can be retrieved with a so-called nymph retrieve. The fish will often follow the fly curiously when it swings across the current, but the moment the fly is given life and darts away, the predatory instincts of the salmon or sea trout will take over and it will make a dash for the fly before it escapes.

> **Release line when the fish takes**
> The secret of solid hookups on fish taking directly downstream is to control your urge to strike. When you feel the fish through the line, release a small amount of loose line. I usually let go of the last loop that I have in my hand. By doing so, you let the fish turn in the current with the fly, and you can hook it when you lift the rod in a steady strike. I have had great success with this method, and catch around 60 percent of all my fish close to my own bank. One reason for this convincing statistic is that I almost always fish close to the bank.

The overhead cast

The overhead cast is an excellent cast and the one you should master with the double-handed rod before you attempt other casts. The physics of the cast are the same as with a single-handed rod, which is why the overhead cast with a single- or double-handed rod is carried out in the same manner. The same phases are followed: the backward movements (lift, actual backcast, and drift) and the forward cast.

Thanks for the fight! A really nice sea trout continues upstream after a short stop ashore. Irigoyen, Tierra del Fuego.

The movements of the arms

The rod must be moved back and forth on the same plane and angled slightly away from the body. This ensures that the line does not hit the rod tip in the forward cast. If the rod is led back and forth in a vertical plane, the line will often hit the rod because gravity will pull down the loop flying forward.

Figure 7-2. Starting position for casting with the double-handed rod.

The right hand holds the top part of the handle in a loose ring-shaped grip, while the left hand holds the lower part of the handle in a similar ring-shaped grip. (See figure 7-3 and read the detailed description of the grip on page 50 for more details.)

The cast is initiated in the starting position shown in figure 7-2. The line is straight downstream in direct extension of the rod, and the tip guide is pointing toward the surface.

The lift is then started by positioning the arms as shown in figure 7-3. The lift is now concluded and the rod is in the front stop. The front stop is roughly translated to an angle of 45 degrees, or as shown on the face of a clock, equal to 1:30, as you can see in the photo. (Check out the illustration of the face of the clock on page 30.)

Notice how the right upper arm is hanging passively, almost vertically, while the right arm is close to horizontal. The left hand grips the lower rod handle, which is supported on the stomach of the caster. These terms of vertical and horizontal are only rough guidelines, because the actual position varies as the body shape of the caster varies. In the photo, note that the natural position for me is to hold my right arm forward a bit; it is not 100 percent vertical, but I still have a right angle between the upper and lower arm and the rod is still at a correct angle.

In figure 7-3, the rod is in the front stop. The next phase is to move the rod to the back stop as shown in figure 7-4. The left hand has pushed the butt section forward, while the wrist of the right arm is bent slightly backward. The right arm can be bent a bit, but the greater part of this movement is made by pushing the butt-cap forward.

Figure 7-3. The rod is lifted to the front stop.

Figure 7-4. The backcast: the butt-cap is pushed forward, which moves the rod into the firing position.

Compare this photo with the previous shots. Notice how the right elbow is lifted while the angle between the upper arm and the lower arm has been closed. The right wrist is now stretched out in line with the arm, which means that the rod is only angled a few degrees more than in the back stop. If the wrist is not stretched out, the rod will end up in an almost horizontal position. This movement of stretching out the wrist will come naturally to most people.

The forward cast is initiated by pulling with the left hand. The upper hand follows and transmits power toward the end of the cast.

In figure 7-5, the drift has been made and the rod is brought to the firing position.

Figure 7-6 illustrates the position of the arms at the front stop of the forward cast. You can see how the left arm has pulled down the butt-cap to its original starting point and that the right arm has returned to a right angle.

The acceleration of the right and left arms must be coordinated correctly. The movement should start with the left arm pulling the butt-cap in place with a relatively calm movement. When this movement is halfway through, the right arm can now push the rod lightly downward to slightly open up the elbow. Around 70 percent of the power is transmitted through the left arm, while the right arm delivers the remaining 30 percent. The effect of this coordinated movement is that the greater part of the acceleration is situated in the last part of the cast, which is of greatest importance for forming the perfect loop.

The overhead cast in practice

The overhead cast in practice at the waterfront is illustrated in the following sequence of photos. The movements are exactly the same as those that show the cast on the lawn, but these photos show the timing of the cast in detail—how the individual movements are initiated and concluded.

The starting position is depicted in figure 7-7. The previous cast has been fished through and the line is hanging straight downstream.

Figure 7-7. The starting position for overhead casting with a double-handed rod.

In figure 7-8, the cast is about to start. The tip guide is pointing in the direction of the line, and the right and left hands are gripping the upper and lower parts of the handle, respectively. The caster is facing in the direction of the line because this cast is made without giving any angle to the line. The position of the feet is important, too, as described in chapter 8.

Figure 7-6. The forward cast: The butt-cap is pulled in place toward the stomach.

In Figure 7-9, the rod has been raised to the front stop. The butt-cap is resting on the stomach, and the right arm is a little above horizontal. Notice how the line is suspended in the air, almost describing a straight line from the tip guide toward the point where the leader is still anchored to the surface. If you hesitate too long in the front stop, the line will drop down in a curving line and become harder to send straight back.

Figure 7-8. The lift: notice the steady handling of the rod during the lift, which will ensure a good backcast.

Figure 7-9. Front stop.

In Figure 7-10, the rod is accelerating from the front stop to the back stop. The rod is flexing forward due to the weight of the line. The leader has now lost its grip on the surface; the whole line and leader combination is on its way backward in a straight movement.

Figure 7-10. Back stop.

This movement is made by the left arm pushing the butt-cap forward while the right elbow is closed slightly and the wrist is bent a bit. Try to make this movement so the right arm bends after the left arm pushes the butt-cap forward. The elbow is closed when the drift is completed.

In figure 7-12, the rod is moved toward the front stop. The left arm is controlling this movement; it pulls the butt-cap toward the stomach, where it rests. In the photo, you can see that the right arm is about to transfer its contribution to the accumulated acceleration by pushing forward. Notice also that the tip of the rod is a bit blurry in the photo because it is moving forward at great speed. The lower part of the rod is only slightly flexed, because the line being cast is relatively short.

Figure 7-11 shows the drift: the rod is on its way to the firing position. The movement is made by closing and lifting the elbow while the wrist is straightened out. The left arm follows, which will lift the rod without giving it any angle toward the water.

Figure 7-11. The drift is completed, and the rod is in the firing position.

Figure 7-12. The forward cast is over. The rod is lowered as the line descends toward the water.

In figure 7-13, the rod has been checked in the front stop. The elbow is pulled back in place and is now in an open angle; the lower arm is in a right angle. The rod is now straightened out completely. The energy from the flexed rod has been transmitted to the line that is rolling forward, forming a perfect loop.

The rod is lowered, gradually following the descending line on its way toward the water's surface.

The Scandinavian Spey cast

When you master the overhead cast with a double-handed rod, you are ready to take on the Scandinavian Spey cast with no angle in the cast. This cast is the foundation for the variations on the Scandinavian Spey cast that you will need during practical fishing. When you are on the river, it may be necessary to compensate for wind or you may need to send the fly in a steep angle upstream or downstream across the current. A certain degree of adaptation is also required for the situations where you need a sinking line, or a shorter or even longer casting belly.

With the number of opportunities you'll have to use the Scandinavian Spey cast, you'll need to practice this cast to perfection. If you do not have running water conveniently close, don't despair. A lake or even a rainwater reservoir may work fine for your casting practice.

The principles for double-handed Scandinavian Spey casting are exactly the same as the ones explained in chapter 5 for casting with a single-handed rod. The cast shown does not have an angle, but in chapter 8 you will learn how the cast can be done at an angle up to 60 degrees. You will also see how subtle changes in the approach during the lift will enable you to give it an even greater angle.

Figure 7-14 shows the starting position—you are facing downstream directly toward the line stretched out in front of you. Support your weight on your right leg, with your right foot pointing toward the water and in front of the other foot. The right foot is also pointing in the direction you intend to cast. When you make the lift, shift your weight to the left foot. Transfer your weight back to your right foot during the forward cast. (Positioning your legs is a very important detail; see chapter 8 for more information.)

When you practice the basics of the Scandinavian Spey cast, you can lock down the line between the handle and the middle finger of your right hand, as shown in the photo on the top of this page. In this way, you can hold the line firmly during casting, the same way as you will when you need to shoot line later on.

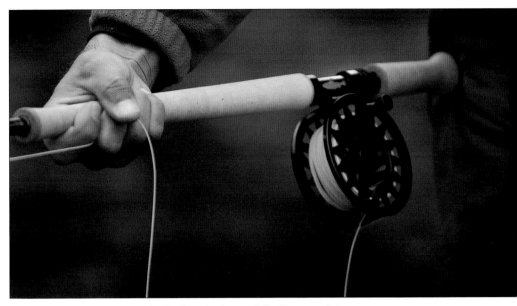

Figure 7-13. The line is locked with the middle finger of the right hand.

Figure 7-14. The starting position for the Scandinavian Spey cast.

Figure 7-15. The lift.

Figure 7-15. A slow and steady lift toward the front stop.

Perform the lift slowly enough so the leader does not loose its grip on the water. The leader should not leave the surface before you start turning your body. This is shown in figure 7-15, where the lift is almost concluded and the rod is caught in the front stop. The line is hanging stretched out between the tip guide and the point where the leader is anchored to the water.

In figure 7-16, the pause is over and the rod is being moved in a flat semicircle directly to the firing position. Remember that there is no back stop in the Scandinavian Spey cast—only the firing position. The tip guide should describe a steadily rising slope on its way from the front stop to the firing position: do not let the tip guide dip on its way; just move it constantly up and back.

This movement is done in practice by leading the right hand out toward your right side and the left hand to the left and out. This will make the rod follow the described course with a steady acceleration. At the same time, the body is turned a bit. Rotate your body clockwise around the hip.

The first part of the cast is controlled by the left hand, which pushes outward toward your left, while the right hand is moved to your side. The last part of the cast brings the rod back to the vertical plane with the right hand, enabling you to start the forward cast the moment the leader touches the water.

Figure 7-16. The rod is moved back in a flat semicircular movement in the backcast.

In figure 7-17, the rod is checked in the firing position. It is no longer out away from you. Instead, it is back in the vertical position with the right hand lifted close to the right cheek. This vertical position is essential for the following forward cast. The torso is rotated a bit toward the right. Notice how the line, in its backward movement, is forming a flat D, the trademark of a well-performed Scandinavian Spey cast.

In a moment, the leader will settle briefly on the surface and the forward cast can be initiated. As mentioned before, the rod must be back in the vertical position and ready to start the forward cast at the exact moment the leader hits the water. If the forward cast is initiated while the rod is still positioned at an outward angle, the loop will be formed sideways, which is a serious error.

Figure 7-17.

In figure 7-18, the forward cast has just started. The rod is flexing evenly all the way to the handle, and you can almost sense how it will give off power from its entire length of carbon. The main part of this movement is made with the left hand, which is pulled into a position where the butt-cap is resting on the stomach. The right hand is only moved forward in the last part of this movement and will transmit about 30 percent of the power needed for the forward cast.

The rod is in the firing position. It no longer shows any angle and is ready to be taken forward in a vertical movement.

Figure 7-18. The leader has landed, the D-shaped loop has been formed, and the forward cast can be initiated.

You can see how the leader is anchored close to the caster in the photo. Many anglers will wait to set the forward cast in motion until the leader is firmly anchored to the surface. This timing is not ideal; at that stage, it will be too late to start the forward cast. The leader should merely kiss the surface: start the forward cast the moment the leader starts touching the surface.

The leader on the surface will hold the cast; the movements of the line are transmitted to the leader. In short, avoid drowning your leader. It will take some effort to loosen the grip of a sunken leader, and to make matters worse, you will create lots of disturbance on the surface.

The large D-shaped loop represents a great deal of energy.

Figure 7-18 (closeup). The forward cast is initiated.

In figure 7-19, the forward cast is almost complete. The left hand has pulled the lower part of the handle back to its position right in front of the stomach, and the cast is completed by simultaneously pushing the right hand out while rotating the torso counterclockwise. The line is on its way forward, but the leader is still anchored to the surface. The rod tip is flexing slightly backward but no loop has formed in front of the tip guide yet.

Figure 7-19. The rod is on its way to the front stop.

In figure 7-20, the forward cast has been carried out and the rod is in the front stop. Compared to the previous photo, the right hand is pushed out a bit farther, while the left hand stays put.

Figure 7-20. The rod is in the front stop. The loop is just starting to take shape.

The leader is still anchored to the surface, the loop in front of the tip guide has been formed, and the line is flying forward at a great speed.

The trick here is to hold the rod steady for the remaining part of the cast. When the line is stretched out in front of the caster, the rod is gradually lowered, following the pace of the descending fly line.

Notice how the rod is flexed slightly forward: this is called the tip bounce. A good rod will show a little tip bounce, but it will also have good dampening qualities, which will quickly steady the bounce. A slow rod will have much more tip bounce, which will result in an unsteady loop. A very fast rod will have a small amount of tip bounce but also poor control during the lift. A good lift is essential to a good Spey cast. The best rod for this cast has a progressive action, which will moderate the vibrations of the rod while it is flexed.

In figure 7-21, the tip bounce of the rod has been moderated. The leader has lost its grip of the surface altogether, and the loop is built up in a perfect torpedo shape.

Notice the high starting point for the cast; this position gives you plenty of time to influence the line as it descends toward the surface. If the upper line is given too much speed, you can lower the rod a bit and avoid having the leader and fly turn over too fast and land with a splash. Remember that the line always follows the tip guide, which means that if the rod is stopped early, the loop will not only be narrow, but it will also shoot across the current horizontally instead of landing with a clumsy splash in front of the angler. A rod raised high in the front stop will facilitate a smooth unfolding of the line and give it plenty of time to descend toward the water.

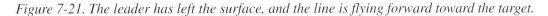

Figure 7-21. The leader has left the surface, and the line is flying forward toward the target.

On shooting the line

When you master the overhead cast and the Scandinavian Spey cast, you will probably feel the urge to put some distance between you and the fly. Fortunately, this is not difficult because you don't have to moderate the movements or the stop positions.

When you do the overhead cast, move the firing position back a bit but maintain the high back stop. You can expand the drift, which will give you a longer stretch of acceleration toward the front stop. You can also place the firing position farther back in the Scandinavian Spey cast. These two casts are similar, in the sense that you can combine the firing position and gain a longer stretch of acceleration by more forcefully accelerating the forward cast. But remember, you have to control the amount of power you put into the cast. You only need enough power to shoot the desired length of line while still stretching the line completely. The art of casting is to cast a long way with a minimum of effort.

If you want to cast more than the length represented by the belly, you need to shoot line. When you do that, the entire belly must be outside the tip guide before the cast is made. This principle applies regardless of whether you use a whole weight-forward line or a line system composed of loose bellies and a coated running line.

Load the rod fully with the entire belly outside the tip guide. The connection between the running line and belly should be 1½–3 feet outside the tip guide, if you wish to do a really long overhead or Spey cast.

When you do a Spey cast this way, the dynamic loop beside or behind you will become deeper. The upper part of the D is longer, which means the amount of active line is longer and will result in a longer cast. Basically, the more line you have activated when the cast is initiated, the longer the wheel (loop) will run. In this way, you can shoot line longer.

If you have 3 feet of running line outside the tip guide at the start of the cast, the loop will start to take shape on the running line. The result is a narrower loop, because the running line is thinner than the belly itself, which in turn means that your cast will reach farther.

The loose line must be released at the exact moment when the loop is forming in the forward cast. If the loose line is sent flying too late or too early, the result will be a poor cast.

Line control in double-handed casting

Unfortunately, there is quite a large amount of loose line to wrestle with when you do a long cast. You can see in figure 7-22 how the loose line is picked up in big loops hanging inside each other. The smallest loop is the one retrieved last and also the first one to fly away. By gathering the line in this way, you can avoid tangles in the loose line when you release the running line. This principle works the best with a floating running line, because it stays on the surface; a monofilament nylon may sink down slightly, giving some resistance when you shoot line.

Another and quite important reason why the last loop should be quite small deals with friction. When you send off a long cast, you must aim for as little friction on the lower line as possible in the initial phase of the cast. As a result, the speed of displacement will be high while the speed of rotation will be low. You can achieve these speeds by keeping the last loops gathered in your left hand and subsequently releasing them first. Small loops will give you less friction, partly because a large part of the line is hanging in the air; the main part of the longer loops is still in the water.

Toward the end of the cast you will need more resistance on the lower line in order to slow the speed of displacement and increase the speed of rotation. The purpose is to make the line and leader unfold, which will stretch the leader and make the fly land delicately. More friction is created on the lower line by the large loop lying on the water, which is the last one flying through the guides.

Figure 7-22. If you hold the loops as shown here, you will rarely get any annoying tangles.

In figure 7-23, you can see how the first and largest loop is held with the little finger of the left hand. Loop number two is held with the ring finger. You may hold a third loop with your middle finger. If you need to do a really long cast, make the loops longer rather than collecting the line four times or more with your left hand. You will inevitably invite tangles if you collect a lot of loops in the same hand.

line down around your middle finger will keep that risk to a minimum.

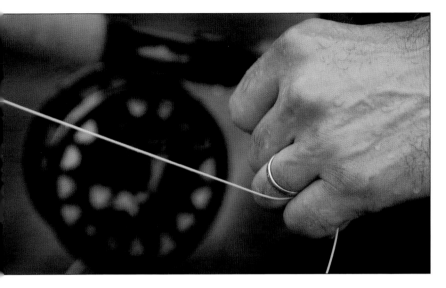

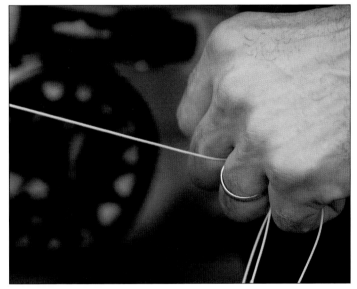

Figure 7-23. The first and largest loop is held by the little finger.

When all the loose line has been retrieved and converted into loops, I grab the running line with the middle finger of my right hand to lock the line firmly during the cast. Nothing is more annoying than having the line slip between your fingers and ruin an otherwise perfect cast. Locking your

Figure 7-24. The loops are released in front of the cast.

Figure 7-24 shows how the right hand secures the line during the cast while the left hand keeps the loose line under control. The right time to let the loose line go is when the loop is starting to take shape. Instead of releasing all the loose line at once, I let the line slip from under the middle finger of my right hand. Then I close my middle finger on the handle again and start releasing the line in my left hand. As the line flies away, I lift or stretch my fingers in the correct order, starting with my little finger, to safeguard against tangling lines, as opposed to letting the line go all at once.

Chapter 8

Advanced Double-Handed Casting

Once you have the left hand Spey correct, all those sweet spots on the wrong side of the stream are suddenly open to you. Pool 29, Mörrum, Sweden.

The way to reach those out-of-bounds spots

This chapter will deal with a number of ways to adapt your casting to enable you to cast and fish optimally under difficult conditions.

The content of the following chapter is the advanced course that follows the different basic casts with a double-handed rod, and it is a precondition that you master those basic casts before you try your hand on these more complicated casts.

First, I will guide you through one of my hobbyhorses: the movements of the body during the cast. You can add extra power and precision to your cast if you try to work with your body during casting.

On most streams and rivers, fly fishers will choose to fish the side that is the most convenient for casting, usually the left bank, if you look downstream. But a stream invariably has two sides, and it is a shame to rule out half the water just because you cannot cast from the "wrong bank." For this reason, you'll want to master the left hand Spey, meaning a Spey cast done with the left hand on top of the grip. Mastering this cast will unlock the stream for you, and you will suddenly be able to fish those out-of-reach sweet spots that were previously hidden from you.

It takes some practice to make your arms, rod, and line work in reverse when you cross the stream to cover new territory. But you will be amply rewarded for your efforts because you can work your fly over water that your fellow anglers are looking at with longing in their eyes.

Next, this chapter will cover the circular cast. This cast may look elaborate and difficult, but it is in fact a very useful cast. By adding a circular movement to the lift, you will be able to angle the line more than is possible with a regular Scandinavian Spey cast. The circular cast will also enable you to tackle heavy upsteam—or downstream—wind.

Finally, I will explain a special technique for fishing a sinking line. It is easier to lift a floating line than a sinking one. For that reason, many fly fishers avoid the sinking line on the stream, but the sinking line is a fine ace to keep up your sleeve for a number of situations because you can present the fly much closer to the fish. And the closer you can get to the fish with your fly, the more likely it is that the fish will take it.

Fortunately, it is just as easy to cast a sinking line as a floating one—if you have the technique right and your tackle is adapted correctly. In fact, because the sinking line is thinner than a floating line, it flies much better and will cut through wind like a warm knife through butter.

A couple of powerful strokes with the tail, and this sea-run brown has regained its freedom. Rio Grande, Argentina.

Use your body

In any kind of sports where an athlete accumulates power, he or she will use the body as a tool. Make a mental picture of a tennis player, a golfer, or a soccer star, and think about how each works his or her entire body for movement control, power, and precision. If these athletes only used their arms while practicing, they would never be successful.

If you study the technique used by competition casters, it is obvious that they, too, use their body to accumulate more power and to extend and enhance the acceleration of the fly rod.

Throughout the years, I have delved into this topic and have tried to find the best, most constructive way to use the body for fly casting. Undoubtedly, the fly cast will improve radically if you let the body follow, support, and enhance the casting movements of the arms.

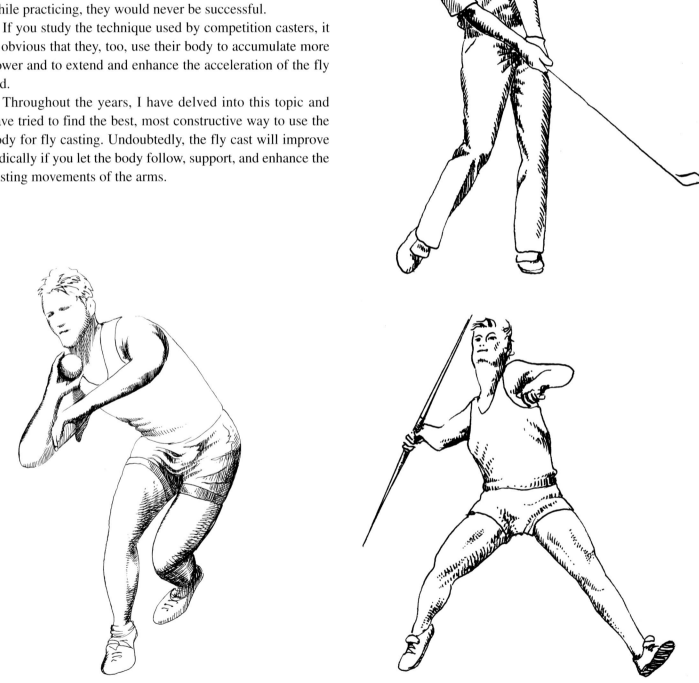

Figure 8-1. The golfer, the shot putter, and the javelin thrower are examples of sportsmen using their body to generate power. The fly caster will benefit if he or she does the same.

Shifting your weight during Spey casting

Chapter 7 dealt mainly with the Scandinavian Spey cast with a double-handed rod, and the focus was on the movements of the rod and the arms. The left and right arm loaded the rod in a coordinated transmission of power. The assumption was that the rest of the body was relatively passive in this movement.

Let's look closer at how the body supports the basic movements of the cast. By mastering these smaller movements, you will get a more powerful cast with better control and presentation of the fly. A harmonious and steady movement makes the rod transmit power to the line in a similarly steady pace. It's not a magic trick at all. In short, this is the procedure.

Shifting your weight step by step

- *Place the foot closest to the water in front of the other foot when you start casting. If you fish from the left bank, your right foot must be in front. If you fish the right bank of the stream, lead with your left foot.*
- *Your foot should point in the intended direction of the cast.*
- *Shift your weight from the front leg to the back leg in the backcast.*
- *Transfer your weight to the front leg in the forward cast.*

The basic principle of the Scandinavian Spey cast, where the line is angled slightly, is depicted in the following series of photos.

In figure 8-2, the caster is in the starting position. Notice how the right foot is in front of the left and is turned toward the water. The posture of the body is also important: the caster is leaning forward slightly in the starting position before the lift is initiated.

The next photo (figure 8-3) shows the rod on its way to the front stop. The lift is done with the arms as well as the body—you gradually shift your body weight to the left foot while the right arm leads the rod to the front stop.

Figure 8-2. Starting position with the weight on the right leg.

Figure 8-3. The weight is shifted to the left leg during the lift.

Figure 8-4 illustrates the backcast in progress. Notice how the weight is still shifted to the left leg by stretching the right leg. This weight change is clearly noticeable by the angle of the right leg.

In figure 8-5 the rod is in the firing position. The line is flying back through the air and the leader is about to land on the surface next to the caster.

Figure 8-4. All the weight is now shifted to the left leg.

Figure 8-5. The line flies through the air. When the leader touches the surface, the dynamic D-shaped loop is formed.

The next two photos (Figure 8-6 and 8-7) are taken in the first half of the front cast. Notice that the right knee is bent and the left leg stretched back out, in order to shift the weight back to the right leg. The coordinated influence of the arms and the body has built up the momentum, which is now clearly visible on the rod.

Figure 8-6. Ready for the forward cast.

Figure 8-7. The forward cast is in progress.

Figure 8-8. The rod has reached the front stop, and the loop is forming in front of the tip guide.

In figure 8-8, the front cast has come to a conclusion and the left leg is stretched a bit farther. The weight distribution on the legs is exactly as in the starting position.

Notice the calm demeanour of the caster and the short tip bounce of the rod, a detail that ensures a minimum of disturbance as the loop is forming.

The method of shifting weight will make the rod work deeper toward the handle, which will use the raw power that is stored in the lower part of the blank. A controlled movement and loading of the blank by working the body will ensure a steady flight of the line throughout the whole cast.

The position of the feet during Spey casting

Let's look at how you shift your body weight during a Spey cast, which is not angled much.

Change the positions of your feet slightly for an angled Spey cast before you start casting. Positioning your feet correctly will help you direct the line during casting even before you start the forward cast. A correct position will also prevent any twisting of the rod during the angling of the cast. Be sure to avoid twisting the rod during casting at all costs; it will capsize the loop, which will make the cast collapse completely. The rod could also twist itself loose in its joints, and it may break.

The drawing below shows the correct position of the feet when the cast is initiated from the left bank. The right foot is in front, pointing in the direction of the cast. Notice how the left foot follows to ensure a firm and steady position.

The position of your feet also determines how much you want to angle your cast. The three positions below illustrate three different angles for the cast across the stream. The arrows mark the direction in each case.

Figure 8-9. The right foot should point in the direction of the cast.

The series of illustrations to the right shows the weight shift during an angled cast with the double-handed rod.

The starting position (at top) shows the weight on the right leg, which is why the left heel is visible. The weight is shifted back to the left leg during the backcast; the left leg is therefore not visible in the two following illustrations. The weight is shifted back to the right leg during the forward cast. The rod should be led in a straight and vertical line during the forward cast. It is important to avoid a slanting loop on the line.

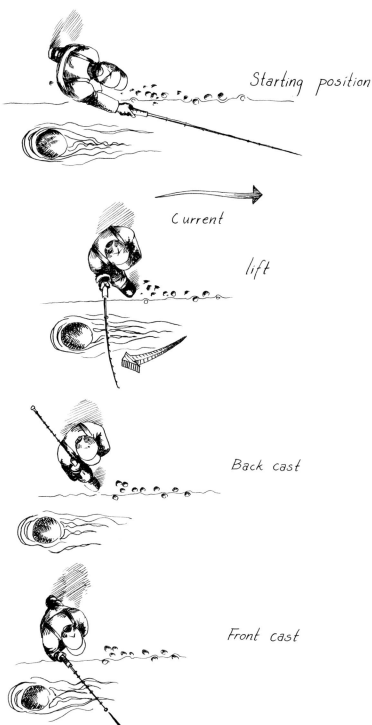

Figure 8-10. The rotation of the body takes place during the lift and backcast.

Notice on the illustrations how the rotation of the body is carried out from the moment the larger part of the rod passes the front stop, up to the point where it reaches the firing position. The rest of the rotation happens during the lift, while the body should not rotate during the forward cast.

This series of photos shows you the angled Spey cast, as seen from an angle behind the caster. It is fairly clear that the right leg is slightly bent during the front stop and the caster is leaning forward a bit.

Towards the end of the front cast the weight distribution of the body supports the movements of the arms, the result being that the arms lead the rod forward in a straight line toward the front stop. Notice how the caster is once again leaning forward slightly.

Figure 8-11. Angled Spey cast: the line is lifted to the front stop.

At the end of the backcast, the weight is mainly on the left leg, and the body is upright and perhaps leaning backward a bit.

Figure 8-13. The rod is in the back position: the body has been rotated.

Figure 8-12. The backcast is initiated: the rotation of the body begins.

Figure 8-14. The forward cast has been completed.

The series of photos on this page shows the same cast, but this time the pictures have been taken downstream from the caster. Because the caster is in the stream, the weight distribution is not visible, but the rotation of the torso is.

Figure 8-15. The caster is facing the line during the lift, but the right foot is already placed correctly, ready for the cast to come.

Figure 8-16. The rod is somewhere near the front stop, and the caster is still facing the river downstream.

Figure 8-17. The backcast is over. The rotation of the body is carried out between the front stop and the firing position, and as a result, the right shoulder is now hidden from the onlooker. The speed was greater at the beginning of the rotation, which means that the last part of the backcast was made with the rod in a position close to vertical in preparation for the forward cast.

Figure 8-18. The forward cast has been carried out. The body does not rotate during the forward cast, because it would be difficult to get the necessary straight line from the firing position to the front stop. The result is a loop that does not slant.

Double-handed casting from the "wrong" side

If you normally hold the rod with your right hand on top and the left hand below, my bet is that you prefer to cover any given stream from the left bank (seen in the downstream direction).

It is only natural that you prefer to cover the stream with casts coming from the "right" side. But it would be a serious handicap to put limitations on your fishing. Essentially, you would be cutting yourself off from all the promising spots that you could cover effectively from the "wrong" side.

Attack the fish from two angles

A good argument for fishing from both banks is that even though you may be able to cover the entire stream with casts from one bank only, you will get the most out of any given river by covering the water from the middle toward the bank.

The most forceful current usually runs down the center of any given stream or river. I usually try to find a way to avoid fishing the hard current running down the middle. If you put a cast across the river, this strong current will grab hold of the fly line and the fish will see it before the fly passes. If you put the fly in the middle of the river at a 45-degree angle, you get a much better drift; the fly will swing from the hard current to the subtle edges that salmon and sea trout prefer.

In some situations, however, the current will allow you to cover a pool just fine from both sides. But salmon and sea trout prefer to stay in the shady side of the stream, so you will need to choose sides according to the sun's position in the sky.

Luckily, reversing your cast and using it from the other bank is quite easy. Of course, it takes some practice to get your arms to do these new movements. But the reward is great: learning to cast from both sides of the river will double your coverage and your opportunities. And you will often have stretches of the river more or less to yourself because only a few can fish the "wrong" side.

Switch arms

You can cope with fishing the wrong bank by simply letting your hands switch places. The left arm is placed on top of the rod handle; the right hand goes below. Otherwise, the cast itself is exactly the same—a mirror reflection of the regular Spey cast.

Figure 8-19. Cast from the right bank with the left hand on top of the handle.

Figure 8-20. The leader is attached to the surface, and the D-shaped dynamic loop is sent forward.

Figure 8-21. As shown, the left hand Spey cast is just a reflection of the regular Spey cast.

Once you have the technique right and you are able to cover the water from the left bank, the time has come to deal with casting that will open the way to fishing along the wrong bank as well.

But before we delve into the particulars of the left hand Spey, I would like to mention a casting technique that can be used as a makeshift solution to fishing the wrong bank.

Crossed hands

It is best, of course, to learn how to cast with the left hand on top, which means mastering the left-handed Spey cast. But if you find yourself on the wrong side of the river and have to get on with your fishing, try this easy way out. Keep the right hand on top and left hand below, while simply moving the cast from your right side to your left: I call this the crossed-hand position.

The advantage is that you can cover the water from the wrong side from the outset. The disadvantage is that the lower hand is more or less redundant in the forward cast. You will need to work more with your upper hand, which may cause a problem even when the cast is angled moderately; the result will be a very limited length of line cast. If you are in a tight spot and need to fish here and now, use the crossed-hand position—but only until you master a genuine left hand Spey.

The starting position when fishing the right bank is shown in the photo. Contrary to the corresponding situation on the left bank, you will notice how the upper hand (the right in this instance) has been drawn considerably in front of the body.

This position is necessary in order to get the right angle between the line and the rod during the lift. If the right arm is not placed correctly during the lift, the D-shaped loop will collide with your body. By placing the arm in front of your body, you can position your leader and make the D in the backcast to your left.

Figure 8-22. The starting position when casting the wrong side of the stream.

At this point the lift is in progress and the rod is on its way to the front stop. Again, notice how the right hand has moved more across the torso and is more stretched out, compared to the similar situation in a normal cast.

Figure 8-23. The rod is lifted.

The leader has just landed. It is anchored to the surface and the forward cast is about to begin. From this position, you can see how the backcast is made by moving the lower hand to the right while the upper hand is moved back to the left. Both hands are raised as they would be during the regular Spey cast.

Figure 8-24. The rod is in the back position.

The forward cast has been completed at this point, and the line is running through the guides. The upper hand has been led forward, while the lower hand is pulling back on the handle. You can clearly see how the lower hand is locked and placed higher than in a regular Spey cast, where the rod is pulled back toward the navel. At this point, you can pull no farther with this hand. Consequently, you cannot add the same amount of power to the cast as in a normal Spey cast. As a result, you are forced to use your right hand more actively during a Spey cast with crossed hands.

Figure 8-25. The front stop of the forward cast. Notice the high position of the left hand.

Left hand Spey

Using a normal (but reversed) hand position rather than a crossed-hand position will give you a greater advantage because casting with crossed hands prevents a powerful pull with the left hand. To make matters worse, it is hard to angle the line much in the crossed hand position. The utility value of the crossed hands position is very limited during practical fishing.

Let's turn to casting with a reversed hand position instead, the so-called left hand Spey.

Learning this reverse cast may be difficult as you give your hands new tasks. Many may feel like they are starting their casting practice all over again. Fortunately, I have a trick to ease the learning process somewhat: when you start to learn this new cast, you can change your grip on the handle slightly.

Normally the left hand Spey is best performed with the left hand holding the handle in a ring-shaped grip. But when you are practicing the reversed hands position, try letting the index finger point in the direction of the blank, making the rod an extension of the index finger. Because the rod will always be pointing in the direction of your index finger, this slight change will allow you to better feel the position of the rod. And it's easier to time the cast if a larger part of the power comes from the upper hand—something I normally advise against.

Figure 8-27. An practice tip is to let the index finger point along the blank.

In the photo below the backcast has started from the front stop and the index finger. The rod is describing a steady but constantly rising curve upward.

Figure 8-26. The left hand Spey is done with the left hand on top.

Figure 8-27 shows the starting position for the left hand Spey. Notice how the index finger of the left hand is stretched out along the line of the blank. Remember, I only advise this adjustment during casting practice. Later, you can practice putting more power into the cast to achieving greater distance, but you should strive to return to a ring-shaped grip on the handle and a relatively larger transfer of power through the lower hand, as in the normal Spey cast.

Figure 8-28: The backcast is in progress.

Figure 8-29. The firing position: when the leader is anchored to the surface, the forward cast is set in motion.

Figure 8-30 depicts the actual forward cast. Compared to a normal Spey cast, the upper hand (the left in this case) is

holding the handle considerably farther up. This position will give you greater control of the rod tip and the cast. When the cast is running smoothly, move your hand farther down the handle.

Figure 8-30. The front position. Notice the high placement of the left hand.

Figure 8-31 shows you the same situation on a larger scale.

Figure 8-31.

A circular cast is a spectacular cast to watch, and it will help you angle the line more during the Spey cast.

The circular cast—not just a circus cast

In traditional downstream wet-fly fishing, the fly is cast at a 45-degree angle where the pressure of the current will make the line and fly fish their way across the stream. Sometimes you will need to cast the line at a steeper angle on the stream, for example, in order to fish the fly faster. If you keep the rod tip close to the surface after such a cast, the fly will swing across the stream at a decent speed.

In other situations, you might want to make the fly fish a deep pool. An ordinary downstream cast will not cause the fly sink much before the pull of the current forces it to swim across. But if you cast at a right angle across the stream, or a bit upstream, while mending the line upstream, the fly will have time to sink before it starts on its way across.

With the normal Scandinavian Spey cast, it is possible to effectively put an angle on the line up to 60 degrees, as shown in figure 8-32. This steep angle is made by turning your torso during the drift of the rod from the front stop to the firing position, as described earlier in this chapter.

If you want to angle the line farther, make a lift with a large circle. It looks impressive, but it is not just artistic showcase casting. If you lift the line through a circle, it will take much

longer before it hits the surface, giving you more time to rotate your torso. The line will follow the movements of the body and will be in a position close to your casting direction in time to deliver the forward cast.

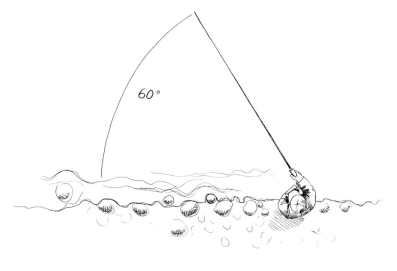

Figure 8-32. A Spey cast can be made with an angle of up to about 60 degrees. The circular cast will open up your ability to cast even steeper angles.

The circular cast has more advantages than just throwing a steep angle into your cast. You will also experience how the cast is happening almost in slow motion, which will buy you time to ease the anchoring of the leader and create an accurate build-up of the dynamic D-shaped loop in the backcast. All of this adds to the precision of the forward cast.

> ### The circle is drawn in the air
> Many casters find that the hardest part of the circular cast is keeping track of the way they need to draw the circle. If you are on the left bank and have your right hand on the upper part of the handle, the rod tip should do a circular movement *opposite* the direction of a clock. I call this cast the Triple C for circle counterclockwise. If you are on the right bank and cast with the left hand on top of the handle (the left hand Spey), the rod tip should be led in a circular movement *with* the clock. I call this the Double C for circle clockwise.

As mentioned before, the central part of the circular cast is the lift, where the line is led in a circle. The remaining parts of the cast, the backcast and the forward cast, follow the principles of the normal Spey cast.

The drawing below shows a circular cast made from the left bank with the right hand on top. The rod tip is moved counterclockwise. It will also give you an idea of the exact stage at which the circle is made.

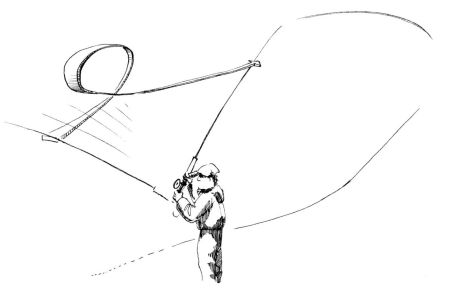

Figure 8-33. When the circle has been drawn with the rod tip, the rod is led to the firing position and the line will follow.

The circular cast step by step
The circular cast is started by moving the rod in a steady movement to a position a bit higher than the normal front stop for a Spey cast. The circle part of the cast is started from this position.

Figure 8-34. The rod is lifted until the circle is drawn.

In the photo below, three quarters of the circular movement has been carried out and the line describes the exact path of the rod tip. Because the caster is standing on the left bank, the circle is drawn counterclockwise as seen from the position of the caster but with the clock when looking at the photograph.

In figure 8-36, the circular part of the cast is complete and the rod is now led to the firing position in a steadily rising curve, as in a regular backcast.

Figure 8-36. The circle has taken the line to a higher altitude, giving the caster time to lead the line and anchor the leader perfectly beside the caster.

In figure 8-37, the backcast is almost complete. You can clearly see that the rod tip has not dipped at any time during the movement by watching the line. The moderate bend of the tip part of the rod indicates that the movement is neither fast nor uncontrolled. You can almost sense that once the line has been set moving, it is merely a matter of leading it with the rod tip.

Figure 8-35. Pure casting aesthetics: the rod tip is the brush painting the circle in the air.

Figure 8-37.

The backcast has been completed with the rod in the firing position while the line is suspended high above the water. The rod should remain in the firing position until the moment the leader is anchored to the surface. The forward cast should begin at that exact moment. You can just see the circular shape on the leader and line in the photo, while the rest of the line toward the tip guide forms a steady curve, which will give the leader a fine attachment on the surface.

Figure 8-38. The firing position.

The rod in figure 8-39 is still in the firing position, and the line is still suspended in the air. The circular shape has vanished. Only the tip part of the line is curving upward. No part of the line is touching the water yet.

Figure 8-39. The leader is pulling up for a perfect landing.

The photo in figure 8-40 was taken the second the leader hit the water. The fly line is forming the characteristic dynamic D typical of a Spey cast. The forward cast known as the Scandinavian Spey cast is now made by partly pushing the upper hand, but mainly pulling the lower hand, back toward the body.

Figure 8-40. The leader is kissing the water in passing.

In figure 8-41, the forward cast has been completed and the cast is angled at approximately 90 degrees without losing its dynamics. In this last photo, the rod is in the front stop, the leader has almost lost its grip on the surface, and the line is rolling forward. *Voilà!*

Figure 8-41. The forward cast sends a narrow loop across the stream.

When the wind is howling, it's nice to know some neat tricks that will keep leader and line on the right course.

Circular casting in the wind

In addition to enabling the fly fisher to angle the cast steeply, the circular cast is also a helpful tool for days when a fierce wind is blowing upstream or downstream.

Most fly fishers have experienced a forceful upstream wind that grabs the line in the backcast and sends it farther upstream than intended—or even into the bushes behind them. And in a downstream wind the opposite occurs: fly line and leader are swept downstream, and it can be hard to persuade the leader to land on the surface and form a dynamic D-shaped loop far enough behind you. In both situations it is hard to send the line across the stream.

However, by putting a circular movement into the lift at an early stage, you can put more energy into the line in the lift and resist the wind more easily when the leader is led in a forceful movement toward the surface. The down stroke movement and the high velocity of the leader (as compared to a traditional Spey cast) means that you will have more control over the anchorage of the leader to the water and be able to build up a nice dynamic D in the backcast.

Casting a sinking line

Fishing with a sinking fly line has often been described as a heavy spring fishing event; a kind of fishing involving long rods, heavy lines, large flies, and forceful movements of the arms. In short, this scenario is not very appealing.

But the whole business gets a lot easier if you use a short 25- to 30-foot sinking shooting head attached to a floating running line instead of a whole sinking line. With the shooting head, you don't need bodybuilding muscles to lift the line to the surface and put it back across the stream.

You also shouldn't confine yourself to fishing a sinking line in the spring season in large rivers boasting powerful current and ice-cold glacial water. If you learn to fish a sinking line, you'll deal yourself a good hand for the whole season because you can often surprise a fish by running the fly close across its nose. Sometimes this trick is exactly the thing to trigger a grumpy old fish, weary from seeing a hundred exact copies skating just under the surface above it.

The splashing roll cast

The hardest part of fishing a sinking line is getting it airborne after the cast has been fished out. But once it is clear of the surface, a sinking line is actually easier to cast than a floating line because it is thinner than a floating line but has the same weight and therefore is less sensitive to the wind. The sinking line is really a dream to cast.

> The lift from the water is the hardest part of fishing a sinking line. Sinking lines hang deep in the water, which makes pulling them out of the water during the lift very difficult. The fly rod simply cannot handle the job of pulling out a deeply submerged line directly for the backcast. To ease this problem, bring the line to the surface before you swing it backward for the backcast.

Many fishermen force the fly line out by doing a roll cast or two before they lift the line clear of the water and send it on with an overhead or Spey cast. In this kind of roll cast, the line and leader do not leave the water in the backcast; instead they drag across the water before the line is cast back out again.

The roll cast technique works, but with one big disadvantage: it will disturb the water and possibly spook fish from under your own bank. Even if you roll the line up close to your own bank, it will still splash. And when the river is high, salmon and sea trout will often stay close to the bank because the current is less powerful there. Learning to lift the sinking line in a less noisy manner can eliminate this disadvantage.

The sinking line is "unscrewed" from the water

Instead of the traditional roll cast, I recommend a casting and lifting technique that makes it possible to practically unscrew the line from the water without any disturbances on the surface. This cast involves an integrated vertical roll cast, where the line is sent out sideways from the caster in the lift. A roll cast is usually performed in the vertical plane, but here the cast is sent from the right and in front of the caster.

The illustrations on this page show how the sinking line is lifted and a sideways roll cast is made to send the line flying. From that point, the line is led backward and the leader is anchored; then you can proceed with a traditional Spey cast.

This technique can also be used when you are fishing a floating line and a fast sinking leader.

The drawings should help you understanding the phases of the cast. To see the cast performed, I recommend the fly casting DVD, *Distance and Delicacy*, which thoroughly explains the cast.

Figure 8-42. Pull the sinking line slowly to the surface by leading the rod to the firing position.

The rest of the belly and the leader are now pulled to the surface by leading the rod to the firing position.

When you cast a sinking line, keep in mind that all movements should be made slower than you would with a floating line. Once it is airborne, a sinking line moves faster than a floating line. If you make rash and fast movements with a sinking line, you will quickly lose control of the cast.

Figure 8-43. The running line is retrieved before the lift so that the back end of the belly is inside the tip guide.

The trick with casting a sinking line is to shorten the submerged part of the line as much as practically possible. Retrieve the line so the back end of the belly is inside the tip guide before the lift is made. This step will make it easier to pull the line out of the water with the double-handed rod.

Figure 8-45. The line is rolled forward and in front of the caster.

A roll cast is made in the vertical plane from the firing position. The rod tip must be checked in a high position on its way forward, so that the line is not sent directly toward the surface but horizontally out in front of the caster.

Figure 8-46. The roll cast in the vertical plane unscrews the line from the water.

Figure 8-47. The line is now in the air, and it is led backward by moving the rod to the firing position.

As soon as the leader is clear of the water and before the line is stretched out in the air in front of the caster, the rod is taken to the firing position. The fly line will follow and descend toward the water.

Figure 8-48. The forward cast is initiated the moment the leader is anchored on the surface beside the caster.

The leader is anchored on the surface beside the caster, the rod is back to vertical, and the line is forming a D behind the caster: the forward cast can begin.

The line flies across the stream, and the only disturbance of the water apart from the anchoring of the leader is when the line once again lands on the water, which is, after all, necessary to get on with the fishing.

This technique is not only useful for casting a sinking line, it can also be used when you have a floating line on your reel. This "unscrew roll cast" is a great help when you have little room to move around between trees and bushes or when you are really close to a fish and need to get the line in the air with the smallest movements possible.

The horizontal roll cast comes in handy in those situations where the cast is fished out and you lead the rod backward to see if a fish is following the fly. You automatically have the rod in the firing position. To get started on a new cast, send the line forward in a horizontal roll cast—you are ready for the forward cast when the leader lands next to you.

This kind of casting, where the lift is combined with a roll cast, adds energy to the cast itself. The whole line becomes active and easier to manipulate.

Your casting technique is seriously tested when you are surrounded by trees on all sides. Pool 32, Mörrum, Sweden.

Chapter 9

Fine-Tuning the Fly Tackle

Fishing for large fish like this sea-run brown will test the fly tackle to the limit, and every small weakness can be catastrophic—not only for you, but certainly for the fish. Irigoyen, Tierra del Fuego.

The difference lies in the details

The time that a fly fisher spends nursing and maintaining his or her fly tackle serves a series of purposes. First and foremost, it ensures that the tackle will work optimally under pressure, for example casting in tight conditions or in the final phase of the fight with a strong fish.

Another important purpose is that when you maintain your tackle, you are fishing! Your mind will wander to the water and you will remember old trips by the stream while dreaming about how the next one will turn out. The fishing trips of the mind certainly have a place in your fishing career as well, especially in the periods where trips are few and far between.

Last but not least, tackle maintenance is an investment. Good tackle does not come cheap, and if you take care of it, it lasts longer.

The fly rod

Many fly fishers twist the rod when they Spey cast, which can cause the ferrules to work themselves loose. Some choose to tape the ferrules on the rod when they fish the same stretch of river for several days in a row. It is a solution, of course, but it is better to correct your casting style if you have a tendency to twist the rod.

Strive to lead the rod back and forth in a straight line. This movement is particularly important in the Spey cast after the rod has done the semicircular movement (see page 102). In this situation, the rod must be brought back to vertical before the forward cast is initiated and it must be moved in the vertical plane instead of forward in a curved movement.

If you cast in a straight line in the forward cast, the rod will be less prone to work itself loose in the ferrules and perhaps break. You will also avoid a slanting loop in the forward cast.

A simple preventive measure is to lightly wax the joints with a piece of a candle. The wax will work as a sort of cement, keeping the ferrules in place. Don't overdo it though; otherwise the rod will be hard to take apart.

Make sure the rod is completely dry before you put in the tube. If it is dirty, clean it with a moist cloth. If your rod was wet when you packed your tackle down by the water, take it out of its bag when you get home and let it and the rod case dry before you store it. Opening up a rod that's been sitting in a wet bag and tube is not a pleasant experience. The bag will become moldy, the cork rings may become discolored, and the varnish covering the lashings of the guides may turn dull.

The guides should be aligned before the parts are pushed together firmly.

When packing up your rod, align the guides before pushing the parts together firmly.

Small particles of salt stick to the rod after a day of saltwater fishing, so it's a good idea to give your rod a quick shower when you return from a fishing trip. Wipe it off with a piece of cloth afterward and let it dry. Dirt and grit can also sit on the rod after fishing in fresh water, typically in the form of dust and algae drying on the blank. The dirt makes it harder to shoot line and forces you to put more muscle into the cast. Wipe the rod with a moist cloth when you're done by the water.

Give the rod a thorough service check once in while. Nothing beats a good polish of the blank and guides with some line conditioner on a piece of cloth. The rod will sparkle like the day it was bought.

The fly line

The fly line is the part of the tackle that requires the most attention. The most important maintenance consists of lubricating and cleaning the line with a line conditioner. Products like car wax and dishwasher detergents have been suggested for this use, but I recommend that you use a product specifically designed for the purpose.

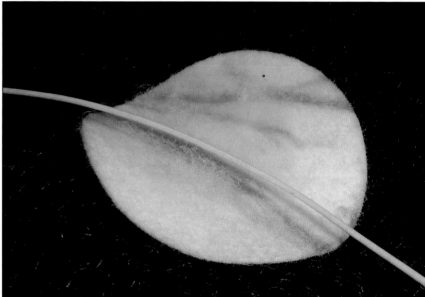

Even an apparently clean line can be covered with a thin layer of salt and dirt, which results in poorer shooting ability.

The fly reel

The fly reel is a simple construction, and it only takes a minimum of maintenance for it to run like new for years on end. But salt in particular can corrode the reel. It sticks to both the inside and outside. So if you're a saltwater fisher, you'll need to do a little more maintenance than freshwater fishers. Take the spool from the frame and rinse each part separately in lukewarm water. Allow the clean reel to dry completely on a towel before you put it away in the reel case. If you are thinking of buying a new reel for fishing coastal waters, keep in mind that a black anodized model is better protected from salt particles than a silver model.

When you rinse a reel in lukewarm water, you dissolve some of the oil and grease in the mechanical parts of the reel. To compensate, wipe the reel with a cloth dipped in acid-free oil. Let the oil rest on the reel for a while so it forms a protective film, then wipe off the surplus oil with a piece of a kitchen towel.

The mechanical parts of your reel may also need a little maintenance from time to time. Look in the manual to see which parts of the reel need oil and grease.

I usually give the line an overhaul after each third or fourth fishing trip. Note that the line should be cleansed *and* lubricated. The easiest way to cleanse and lubricate the line is to pull it through a cloth coated with a line conditioner. When you see a couple of black dirt lines on the cloth—dirt from the line—you can see for yourself that your effort is not wasted. Notice also how smooth the line is afterward. In addition to giving the line better shooting qualities, you also extend its lifespan with a regular cleansing and lubrication. While you are giving the line a treatment, you might as well polish the blank and guides of your rod.

If you don't use a large arbor reel, it is also important to stretch the line before you start fishing. You do this by stretching the line by hand, yard by yard; the process is quicker than it sounds. If you are fishing with a fellow angler, you can help each other by stretching the line to its full length, grabbing opposite ends, and applying steady pressure on the line for 20–30 seconds. If the temperature is low, however, take care not to stretch the line in a sudden jerk; you may damage and crack its coating.

A heavy sea-run brown taken on a leech fly in the darkest night. Irigoyen, Tierra del Fuego.

The backing sits underneath the fly line. It is a good idea to check it for flaws and damages once a year, and spool it back on. Reel the backing back while applying steady pressure and preferably with crossed turns on the spool, as on an open-spool spinning reel. These things in combination will prevent the backing from slicing into itself during a steamy run of your dream fish, with a blocked reel as the result.

Leader and tippet

Because the leader is typically the weakest part of the equipment, you should spend extra attention on this part. In short, your leader should always be in perfect condition. The leader will invariably receive a fair amount of bruising from snagging the bottom or jamming between boulders in the current or along the shore. Check the leader regularly to make sure it is in mint condition. Check the polyleaders as well; the loops on these should be without flaws.

When you tie the tippet to the end of the tapered leader yourself, use only fresh nylon. Leader material will deteriorate if it is kept in a moist pocket of a fishing jacket throughout the season. Always take care to keep the leader material out of direct sunlight. The UV rays of the sun will break down nylon over time.

Modern nylon has many interesting qualities. One of them is that different makes of nylon do not work equally well together. Make sure that the nylon you use goes with the knots you tie. This subtle nuance becomes especially important if you tie different types of nylon, and connecting different types of nylon is especially critical when you use the surgeon's knot or the double blood knot. If you aren't familiar with nylon combinations, use the loop-to-loop principle. The next chapter describes these knots.

Always remember to stretch the nylon before use. This goes for newly bought tapered leaders fresh from the pack as well as leaders that have stayed on the spool for a long time. The leader will eventually stretch out by itself when you cast it, but there is no reason to start the day off casting on a curly leader.

You'll also want to moisten the leader before you take the first cast. When the leader has sucked up some moisture, it will stretch better and fish well from the very first cast.

Chapter 10
Good Knots

The loop-to-loop connection is a clever and functional way to set up the line system.

In this chapter, we will look at the knots and splicing you need before and during fishing. The knots are used to connect the tackle, from spool to tippet end, which means connecting the backing to the spool of the fly reel and coupling the backing, running line, and fly line through the loops and then through the leader to the fly, which is tied to the tippet.

Developments, experiments, and new ways to do things are usually good, but when it comes to knots, you'll want to be conservative. Fishing magazines and books regularly introduce new knots or show how old knots have to be tied in a new way. But those often go wrong, mostly because fly fishermen cannot resist the urge to experiment and tamper with the instructions and maybe give the knot one more turn than necessary in hopes of making the knot in question even better than before. But why not do the knots as simply as possible? My father taught me to tie the knots described in this book many years ago. These knots are simple to tie and they have remained that way.

Throughout the years, I have seen many poor ways to connect lines and leaders. Poor connections can impair the cast, and this is bad enough, but the worst part is that many fish are lost because knots and loops are not made properly. The funny thing is that when an improperly or poorly made knot breaks, the comment invariably is that the fish was so strong it simply tore the knot apart.

In short, it does not make logical sense to travel thousands of miles, to fish for days or weeks for the fish of your dreams, and then when that fish takes, to lose it just because you did not spend a quarter of an hour to make sure that all loops and knots in your equipment were properly made.

Practice knots at home

Avoid at all costs experimenting with new and interesting knots when you are on the water. Practice at home instead, so the knots are perfect every time. If you tie a dubious knot and you question its strength, retie it! All the turns in the knot should be neat and bunched up nicely. A knot that looks dubious will never last in the long run anyway.

Also, remember that there is a difference between you applying pressure on a knot once or twice when you test it for strength and a strong fish applying constant pressure during a long fight.

If you belong to the very meticulous category of fly fishers, you can test the strength of a knot with a spring balance. Remember, the key is the breaking strain of the wet knot, so test the knot through prolonged steady pressure as well as sudden jerks.

Knots from backing to tippet

You need a number of knots to connect reel, backing, running line, fly line/belly, leader, and tippet. There are hundreds of knots you could use, but the knots in this chapter are those that I have used during the last 30 years of practical fishing and found to be useful. In short, they have never let me down!

A darning needle, a filed-down syringe needle, a threader, and knot glue belong in the knot tier's toolbox. If you want extra-secure knots, you will need a thread bobbin with fly-tying thread.

The knot tier's toolbox

It is a good idea to keep your tools for knot tying and splicing in a small box. Label the box in clear writing according to content. With this box at hand, you will always have the things you need in their proper place when you need them, and you will be ready to fine-tune your tackle no matter where you are. The box could contain any of the following: scissors, pliers, a small tube or bottle of knot glue, Aquaseal, fly-tying thread and bobbin, needle, threader, a syringe needle with a filed-down tip, a darning needle (for nail knots), and 0.014-inch nylon (to peel off the fly-line coating).

Another tip is to bring Xerox copies of the knots or loops. Fold the photocopies to fit in your tool box, so you always have the drawings for support.

Knot between backing and spool

You can choose between two types of backing. The classical spun Dacron is still the most commonly used type, but new types with a smaller diameter and higher breaking strain are gaining ground. They are called *gelspun* or microbraid backings, depending on the make, and they resemble Fireline or other braided "super lines" used for spin fishing. You have to use different kinds of knots with these types of backings than you would with a Dacron backing. The recommended knot for such lines is usually stated on the package. It is important that these new types of lines be reeled in with something resembling a cross lay up. Otherwise the line may cut into itself when the fish sets off on a long run. If that happens, you can wave goodbye to your fish.

The spool axis knot

This knot is a classical one for use with spun Dacron. Pass the backing round the spool axis once before the knot is tied. Make a simple overhand knot around the main line, and pull it up semitight. Make sure that at least 4 inches of line stick out from the knot.

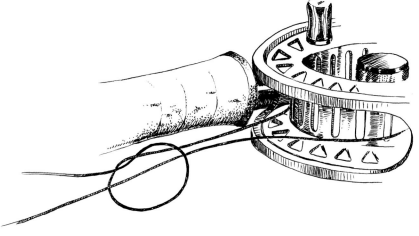

Figure 10-1.

Now, tie a simple overhand knot on the loose end. This one is firmly tightened and the remaining line is cut off, leaving a small tail.

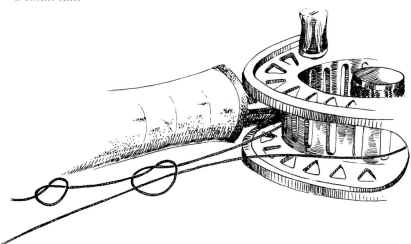

Figure 10-2.

The inner knot is then tightened, and the outer knot will act as a stop for this knot. Tighten up completely so the backing slides in against the spool. It must be tight enough to resist rotation.

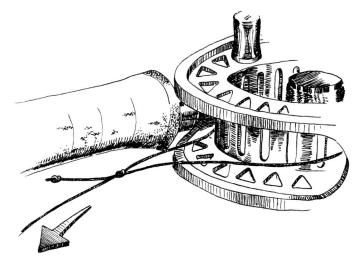

Figure 10-3.

Uni-knot as a spool axis knot

The Uni-knot, which is also called the Duncan loop, is an alternative to the spool axis knot. This knot is commonly used to tie the fly to the tippet, but it works just fine to tie the backing to the spool axis, especially when you use one of the new types of backing. These inelastic lines have a hard and smooth surface, and the spool axis knot will not work with these because the two overhand knots may slip.

When you do a Uni-knot, pass the backing once around the spool axis so the two lines are parallel and held with the left hand. Using your right hand, form a large loop with the loose end and hold it with your left hand.

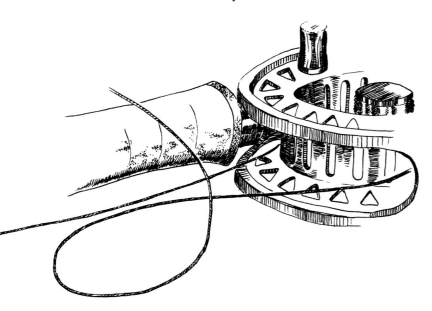

Figure 10-4.

Put the loose end through the loop and around both lines with your right hand. Do at least five turns.

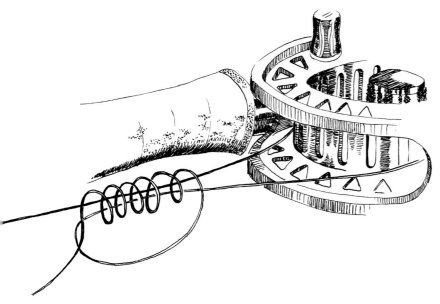

Figure 10-5.

Tight the knot with a steady pull of the loose end while you keep hold of the basis of the knot with your left. Let go of the knot when it is completely tightened.

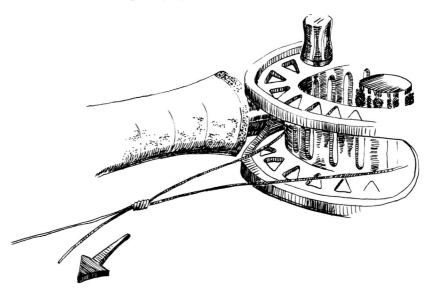

Figure 10-6.

Cut the loose end close to the knot. Now, pull the main line so that the knot is close to the spool. Tighten it up so the backing is firmly locked down and cannot turn. I prefer to let half an inch of the loose end remain, especially when using *gelspun* backing. You can make a simple overhand knot on the end, which will ensure that the knot does not slip.

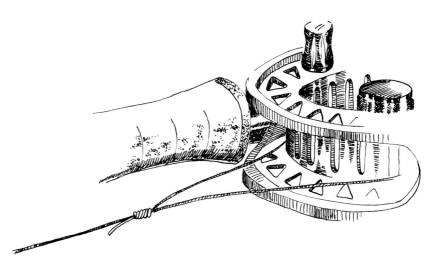

Figure 10-7.

Loops on spun backing

If the backing is spun Dacron, you can connect it to the fly or running line in one of two ways: either by the loop-to-loop system, where a loop is spliced on the backing and running line/fly line, or with a needle knot (see page 177).

Let's look at a very strong, yet elegantly spliced loop. Unfortunately, you can only make this on certain types of spun backing because the backing has to be hollow to work with this splicing. Some types incorporate an integrated thread woven crosswise, which makes it impossible to splice.

The first step is to make a threader out of thin wire, such as the thin copper wire found in electrical wires. Fold the thin copper thread. You can also buy a threader designed for the purpose, like the one in the drawing below, but the home-made one is just as good.

The threader is inserted in the Dacron line approximately 12 inches from the end (figure 10-8). The distance depends on how large you want the loop to be. The threader is led 1–1 ½ inches through the hollow Dacron and then out through the side. Pass the end of the Dacron through the threader as shown in the drawing below.

When you pull back the threader, the Dacron will follow through by itself. If it jams, help it along by pushing the Dacron in the opposite direction of the pull.

Adjust the size of the loop, and pull the Dacron so it is nice and even.

Now repeat the process with the threader, so the Dacron is threaded into a new piece of 1–1 ½ inches The end of the threader should emerge approximately ½ inches behind the previous exit hole (figure 10-9, lower drawing). Pass the end of the Dacron through the threader again, and pull.

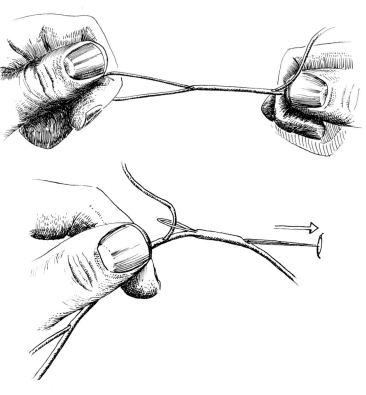

Figure 10-9.

The Dacron has now been led through itself in two places, separated by a ½-inch section where it runs parallel to itself.

Cut the loose end, smear a drop of superglue on it, and draw it back into the core of the Dacron when you tighten the loop. The elegant and very strong loop is now completed. Some knot tiers choose to secure the loop further by sewing the connection with a needle and fly-tying thread, but I don't.

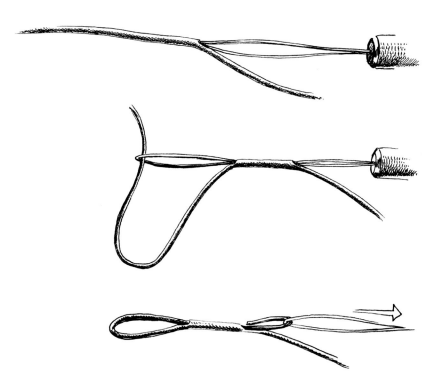

Figure 10-8.

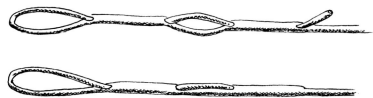

Figure 10-10.

The loop-to-loop connection should be able to pass through the guides on the rod without any risk of blockage.

Loops on fly lines

It is useful to splice loops on both ends of your fly line so you can make loop-to-loop connections with the backing on one end and the leader on the other. This knot is basically two loops threaded into each other, and it can be compared to a reef knot, which is a very strong connection. If you use a shooting head system, you can couple the bellies to the running line with the loop-to-loop principle. A polyleader can also be connected to a loop.

As you can see, there are many good reasons why you should learn how to splice loops on your fly lines. It takes a bit of practice, but it's not impossible. Let's look at how it is done.

You can make loops on any fly line with a woven inner core that is thick enough to work with. You can whip a ready-made braided loop onto the fly line instead of splicing one if the core is too thin. Use fly-tying thread with a good breaking strength and finish the turns with a series of half hitches. Secure the whipping with a coating of glue. Most waterproof glues can be used, as long as they are flexible. If they are not, the glue might peel off or cause the line to break. Aquaseal, which is used for repairing waders, is excellent. You can also buy small tubes of special knot glues that have the advantage of drying within minutes.

> **Warning!**
> If you mount a ready-made braided loop on your fly line, stay well clear of the small plastic sockets sometimes supplied with the loop. If you mount the loops with the sockets, you have no certainty that they will stand any kind of pressure.

I have seen fly fishers giving in to the easy solution and trusting the plastic sockets for their fly lines. Unfortunately, the weakest part of the tackle is often bound to show itself in the most critical phase of the fight, which is the landing. Losing a fish that way will leave you with a hollow feeling inside.

Think of how much effort it takes to make the fish take the fly. Maybe you have even traveled a long way in the pursuit of the fish of your dreams and paid a considerable sum of money while preparing yourself in every conceivable way. When your rod finally bends satisfyingly forward, you don't want all your efforts to end with a sour taste in your mouth, just because you chose the easy solution.

The fist step of making a loop on the fly line is to peel off a piece of the coating on the line. How much coating you need to strip off depends on the length you need for the loop. If you make a loop on the running line you need to make the loop large enough to pass the fly reel through when the line is doubled. You only need to peel off about 4 inches when you make loops on the shooting head.

You can dissolve the coating with acetone, but that is fairly toxic. It is easier to peel off the coating with a piece of mono-filament line with a diameter of around 0.014 inch. The nylon line should be thin enough to cut through the coating, but strong enough to withstand the pressure when you pull the coating off.

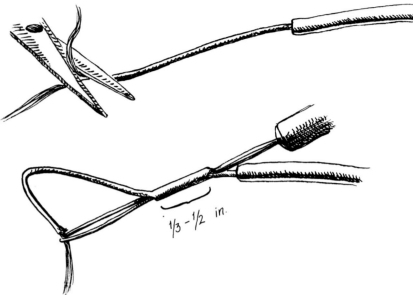

Figure 10-12.

Now catch the core with the threader or folded wire and run it back through itself. You do this by running the threader through half an inch of the core, from the point where the coating ends, as in the drawing above.

The easiest way to do this is to run a needle through the core to prepare the way for the threader. It is easier if the coating is bent where the needle has been inserted and the threader goes in. When the threader is run through the core, pass the reduced core tip through the threader loop and pull it back through the core. The loop has now been shaped.

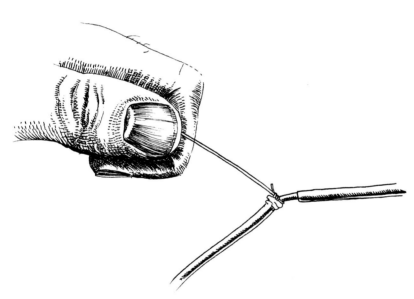

Figure 10-11.

Do a simple overhand knot or a lure knot around the fly line and tighten. Now pull off the coating in a single, steady pull (see the drawing above). If the coating is hard to peel off, use pliers when pulling the line. That way you avoid cutting your fingers when you put some muscle into the process. You can only remove the coating from a small piece of fly line at a time, so you need to repeat the process three or four times.

The next step is to use a needle to fray the topmost half inch of the core. The stripped, frayed core is separated in half and one part is cut off, as shown on the drawing above. The reason for splitting the core is that it will enable you to pull back the remaining core through itself. You cannot do this unless you reduce the thickness of the core.

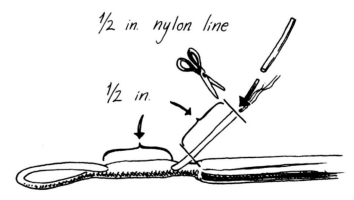

Figure 10-13.

Use the woven structure of the core to secure the loop. As you can see in the drawing, you attach a piece of monofila-ment nylon to the piece of core pulled through: when it is pulled back, the core will be under a subtle but constant pressure. The pressure increases the more you pull the loop.

As you can see in the drawing, the length of nylon inserted should correspond to the stretch where the core is doubled up inside. A little over 1 ½ inches will do it. Depending on the thickness of the core material itself, use nylon between 0.013 and 0.016 inch.

You now need a fast-drying knot glue, available in tackle shops. Add a bit to the nylon piece before it is inserted in the stump of core sticking out of the core. The bit of core is also smeared in glue, before you retract it into itself.

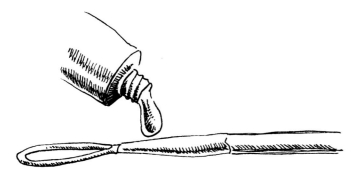

The last step is to add glue to the outside of the loop. Check that everything looks right before you do this. If you have even the slightest doubt about the loop, redo the whole thing.

Now cover the joint in knot glue to make a smooth and even transition from fly line to loop. The loop will be ready to use in a short while. You can make an even smoother transition between the line and the loop if you use a thicker flowing glue like Aquaseal. If you don't, you might get an annoying edge between the two (line and loop) that has a tendency to catch the rod guides when you strip the line.

Knots and loops between fly line and leader

The most important function of the leader in the cast is to counterweight the upper line against the lower line. The leader also plays a decisive role in the way the fly moves and how it is presented to the fish. Varying fishing situations may demand different types of leaders. Polyleaders are popular today for almost any type of fishing and with good reason. They are durable and easy to change. This means that you can change the sinking rate of the leader in a few moments and present the fly exactly where you want it: right under the surface, in the middle of the water column, or deep down at the bottom.

The core of any polyleader is copolymer monofilament nylon. The diameters of the polyleaders vary, depending on the breaking strain. Different types of coatings are used in the manufacturing process, in order to get different sinking

A salmon has followed the dry fly several feet before taking it. It doesn't get more exiting than this. Bonaventure, Canada.

rates. A floating polyleader has a polyethylene coating, while the coating of an intermediate polyleader consists of polyurethane. Sinking polyleaders have a coating of polyurethane mixed with tungsten powder. The more tungsten in the mix, the faster the leader sinks.

You come across situations where the tapered leader is preferable: amongst other things, for fishing small flies in the surface. The best way to attach a nylon leader to the tip of the fly line is with a needle knot, which is described on the next page. The leader will seem like a direct extension of the line with the needle knot. At the same time, this knot is very compact and efficient, and will make little disturbance on the surface when used in conjunction with a floating line.

You can also make a loop such as a perfection loop on your leader (see page 178), which makes it easy to switch between nylon leaders, as with polyleaders. Unfortunately, the loop on a fly line with a Dacron core often sits a bit askew, because the loop on the nylon leader is stiffer than the soft Dacron. You can attempt to straighten the loop out a bit, by giving the loop on the thick part of the leader a careful squeeze with a pair of flat pliers, which will enable the soft Dacron core to hold the connection in place.

The needle knot is also useful if you wish to connect the fly line and backing with a knot instead of using the loop-to-loop method.

A large salmon gave the tackle a thorough testing—any weak spots in leader or knots would have had fatal consequences. Grand Cascapédia, Canada.

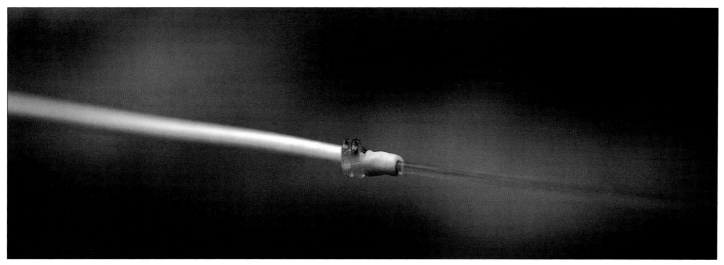

The leader will be a natural extension of the fly line with the needle knot.

The needle knot

Make a needle knot by inserting a small needle ⅕ inch up and through the tip of the fly line and out though the side. Hold the needle with a pair of pliers and heat the needle over a flame.

Pull out the hot needle to leave a small hole behind in the fly line. If the needle is too hot, the line will melt completely and you will have to start from scratch. Try again after cutting off the melted part of the fly line, heating the needle a little less this time.

Insert the tip of the leader through the hole in the side of the line and pass it through the tip. Pull the entire leader through until about 6 inches are sticking out of the hole. If the leader is hard to pull through, moisten it a bit. This process is easier than pushing the thick part of the leader through the line tip.

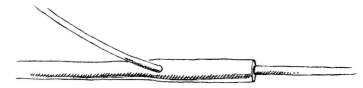

Figure 10-14.

Now, choose a tube used for tying tube flies or a heavy syringe needle from a pharmacy or veterinary clinic. The latter type of needle is better because the diameter is larger and easier to work with. Remember to file down the syringe needle tip before you start. Place the tube parallel to the fly line and leader, just below the place where the leader comes out the side of the fly line.

Hold the fly line and nylon leader with your left thumb and index finger, and turn the leader five times around the fly line, the tube, and itself. If the leader is any thicker than 0.020 inch, turn the leader only three times. Move the left hand forward a bit, so your fingers hold all the turns securely.

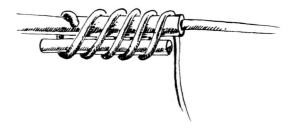

Pass the loose line at the end through the tube, and pull gently. Your grip should loosen gradually as you feel the turns fall into place.

When the knot is just about there, pull the tube off the leader. It is important to grab the turns of the leader with your index finger and thumb, otherwise the turns might displace themselves. If the turns are not bunched up nicely, your work is wasted.

The knot is now tightened enough to keep the turns from moving, but do not tighten it too much because you need to slide the knot down the line to the correct position. The front turn of the knot needs to be adjacent to the point where the leader goes into the fly line. When the knot is at that point, tighten it completely by pulling the loose end with pliers. The finished needle knot, with all the turns are neatly bunched up next to each other, looks like the one below. You can cover the knot in knot glue or Aquaseal to make the transition between the fly line and leader extra smooth and harmonious. Smear a little onto the knot, and turn it while you spread the glue with a moist finger.

Figure 10-15.

Loops on nylon leaders

A good way to connect two pieces of nylon in a leader is to use the loop-to-loop principle. I hardly ever use anything else for salmon fishing. The advantage is that you can connect two pieces of nylon with differing diameters in a simple way.

The surgeon's loop

The surgeon's loop is the fastest and easiest loop to tie. The knot is made by doubling the nylon and making a simple overhand knot followed by yet another turn, making it ideal for heavier lines. Use a knot with three turns for lines thinner than 0.012 inch. A knot with two turns for heavier lines is shown on figure 10-16.

Adjust the size of the loop by pulling the ends before the knot is tightened. The smaller the loops are, the harder it is to close them: if you connect two small loops, they will have a tendency to open up when the lines are slack. Two large loops, on the other hand, stay where they are when you draw the nylon lines. A knot with a diameter of about an inch is just about the right size and will close like it should.

Holding onto both ends makes the knot very tight; you can use a pair of pliers with rounded edges and pass it through the loop and then tighten up the knot. When the loop has been thoroughly tightened, cut the loose end close to the knot. This part is important, because you can be sure that even a tiny stump of line sticking out is sure to catch the leader in the cast.

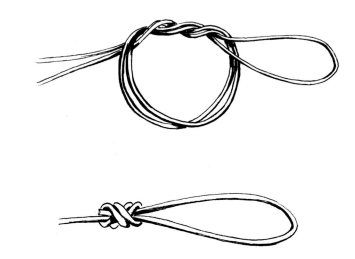

Figure 10-16.

Perfection loop

The best loop is a perfection loop. It takes a little longer to tie, but it is extremely strong, and when tied right, it is beautifully pear shaped.

Start by holding the line between your left index finger and thumb. Pass the loose end behind itself and hold it between your two fingers so a 1-inch diameter upright eye is formed (see figure 10-17).

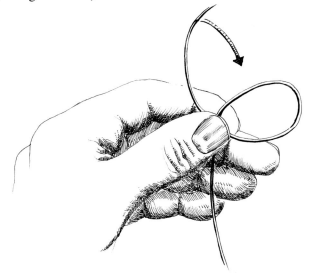

Figure 10-17.

Pass the loose end around the upright eye and back between your two fingers. Your loop now has two eyes: the first eye is upright and the other lies flat next to your thumbnail. The size of the second eye determines the size of the finished loop. Pass the loose line end down between the two eyes, and hold the loose end down again.

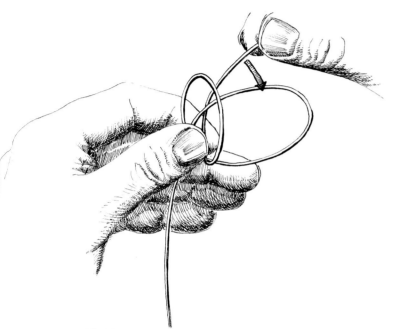

Figure 10-18.

The second eye is now passed through the first one by sticking the right thumb and index finger through the first eye and pulling the second through.

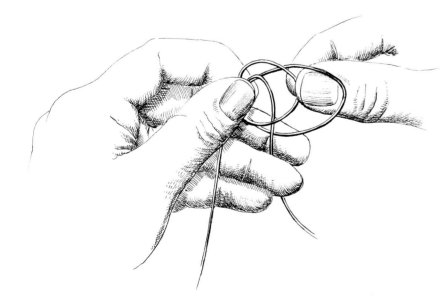

Figure 10-19.

The loop is now finished, and you can cut the loose end close to the knot. If you do it right, the loop will have a characteristic pear shape.

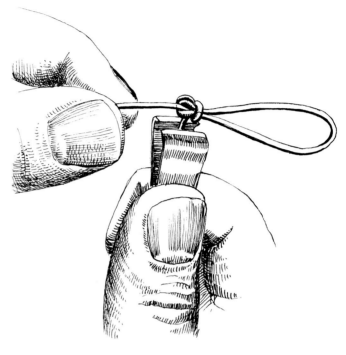

Figure 10-20.

Connecting nylon lines

I prefer to tie different pieces of nylon with a solid knot, instead of using loop connections, for light single-handed fly fishing. I make sure to use leader material of the same kind for the tippet as I used in the tapered leader. Nylon materials from different manufacturers will often work against each other. If one line is harder than the other, for example, it may damage the other.

Some fly fishers prefer to use fluorocarbon, which is a very strong and slow-sinking tippet material. But this material has a couple drawbacks. First, it deteriorates very slowly when left outdoors. Second, you will need special knots for fluorocarbon. The material is so tough that you risk damaging your teeth if you attempt to bite off the loose end when you tie a knot. For these reasons, I do not use fluorocarbon at all for fly leaders.

Surgeon's knot

The surgeon's knot is by far the easiest knot to learn, and it works well with leader material thinner than 0.010 inch (1X). Double up the lines with a length of about 4 inches, and then make a simple overhand knot on the folded line (figure

A small salmon fly tied on a treble is tied to the tippet. The surgeon's loops ensure that the fly can move freely and enticingly in the current.

10-21). Hold the two ends tightly so the lines are parallel. Make another turn. The knot will then consist of two turns, which will create a figure 8 shape that connects the lines in extension of each other. (See figure 10-22.)

Figure 10-21.

Tighten the knot by holding the loose end and the main line and applying steady pressure (figure 10-22). Moisten the knot slightly before it is tightened completely. Trim the loose ends so the leader does not snag on itself.

Figure 10-22.

Double blood knot

The double blood knot is a classic knot especially suited for heavy nylon lines thicker than 0.010 inch (1X). Start by crossing the two lines and holding the point where the lines cross with your left thumb and index finger. Turn the loose end three or four times with your right hand, and pass it under the cross. Now change hands so the knot is in your right hand.

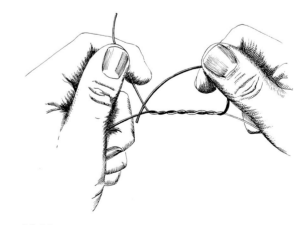

Figure 10-23.

Using your left hand, turn the other loose end three or four times in the opposite direction around the main line. Pass the end under the cross where the other end sticks out. It is important that the two line ends are passed through from opposite directions (see figure 10-24).

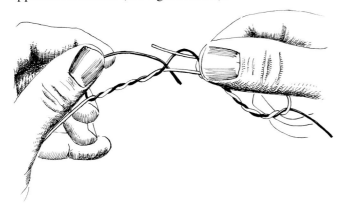

Figure 10-24.

Now tighten the knot by pulling the main lines lightly. Remember to moisten the knot.

If the stumps are too short, they might slip from their place. Use long ends, around 4 inches, when you practice tying this knot. When you've mastered the technique, you can shorten the ends a bit.

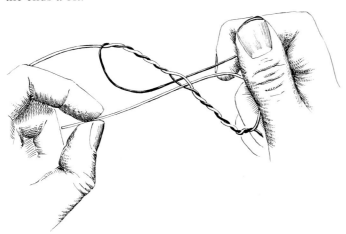

Figure 10-25.

Cut the loose ends close to the knot so the leader does not catch the stumps.

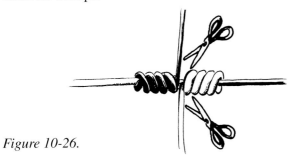

Figure 10-26.

Fly knots

The knot between the tippet and fly is the one you use most frequently. A couple knots have distinct advantages depending on the fly you use. I prefer to tie the fly in a loop, if possible. A loop will give the fly the ability to move in the current.

I will run through the four knots I use most frequently. Remember, by the way, to stick the fly into something other than the fingers when the knot is tightened up at the end!

Simple surgeon's loop

This loop is very simple, and it will make a small dry fly or nymph move enticingly at the tippet end. The loop is small enough to prevent the fly from hanging up on itself yet large enough for the fly to move freely.

Figure 10-27.

Tie the knot as the previously described surgeon's loop (see page 178), but thread the fly onto the tippet before the line is doubled up.

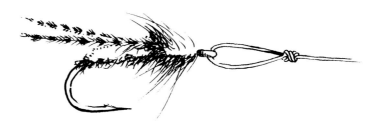

Figure 10-28.

Adjust the size of the loop after you have tied the knot but before it is tightened completely. The advantage of this loop is that it is quick to tie yet strong enough for this kind of light fishing.

Nonslip mono loop

This knot is ideal for heavier fishing for salmon and sea trout or for smaller flies at the end of a thin tippet. The loop takes a little longer to tie, but it is very strong.

Start by making a loose overhand knot on the tippet where the fly will be threaded. Pass the tip of the leader back through the overhand knot, as shown in the drawing below. Tighten the overhand knot slightly, but not so much that you cannot pass the line through again.

Figure 10-29.

Now turn the loose end around the main line three times.

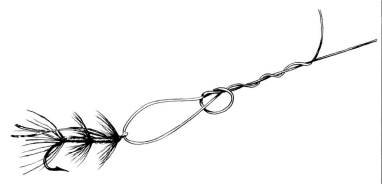

Figure 10-30.

Pass it through the overhand knot one last time. Make sure that it goes back through the same loop it came from.

Figure 10-31.

Now tighten the knot completely. You'll need some practice to make the loops small enough, but it is worth the effort.

Figure 10-32.

Knots for tube flies

When I use small tube flies on metal tubes, I let the hook hang loose behind the fly. The wing of the fly will steer the loose hook in the current, and it will always turn upward with a leg of the hook on either side of the wing. The advantage this provides is that the salmon is then always hooked in the upper jaw, which is the best place to hook a salmon. Since I started to let the hook hang loose behind the tube fly, I have lost practically no salmon on this type of fly! Another advantage with the upturned double hook is that you can fish the fly really close to the bottom without snagging.

I always use small trebles for plastic tubes and also hitch tube flies. It is easy to think that a large treble will give you a better hookup rate than a small one, but in my experience it is the other way around. The smaller treble will hook the salmon with all three hooks. But the treble must be held in place with a tube socket to ensure that the hook will get a good hold in the mouth of the fish at the moment it takes. Use a piece of soft, plastic tube a little over half an inch long. The plastic tube must fit around the back end of the tube tightly when you push it in order to stay there. The soft plastic tube ensures that the hook is always in direct extension of the fly and that the fly and hook separate the first time the fish jerks its head when it is hooked. This means that the fish cannot use the tube fly as a lever to shake out the hook.

The salmon could be practically everywhere on this stretch; the fly is parked for a few seconds over each promising spot. Núpsármót, Miðfjarðará, Iceland.

Uni-knot

I use this knot for tube flies tied on ¼- to ½-inch copper tubes and double hooks. A strong Uni-knot takes the place of a loop or steering knot.

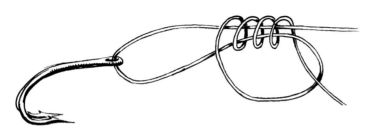

Figure 10-33.

The Uni-knot is a relatively simple knot to tie. Thread the tube fly onto the leader first and then the hook. Hold the hook in your right hand, and pass the end of the line down between your right index finger and thumb. The loose end has now formed a loop parallel to the main line. Pass the loose end through the loop, and turn it three or four times around the main line. Tighten lightly. Moisten the knot before tightening it completely, and cut off the line end. The knot is finished, and the tube fly can be slid down to its correct position.

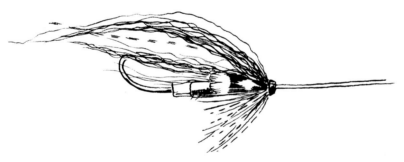

Figure 10-34.

Simple turtle knot

For some fishing situations, a steering knot will, without doubt, be the best choice. One example is salmon and sea-trout fishing in a very turbulent current, where a fly tied on in a loop will move through the water much too erratically. The simple turtle knot is a classic among steering knots.

The hook eye needs to be angled steeply up or down to make the knot work well, and it also has to have a wide profile, which will make the knot cling around the base of the eye, like a necktie. If the eye of the hook is not angled enough, or if the eye is very slim, you risk the knot slipping off the eye.

Start by threading the fly onto the leader. If the hook eye points upward (as in the drawing), pass the line through from

below. If the eye points downward, it's the other way around. Tie a simple overhand knot on the line.

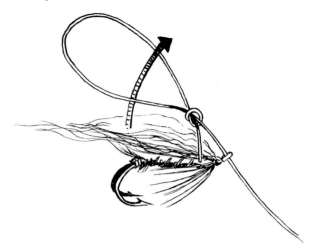

Figure 10-35.

Tighten the overhand and pass the line through the loop, and then put the loop round the neck of the hook and tighten.

Figure 10-36.

When you have tested the knot thoroughly by pulling on the leader, cut the end as close to the knot as possible so it does not show. If you choose to let the line end hang down alongside the fly, you won't need to cut the end at all.

Figure 10-37.

As I mentioned before, the angle on the eye must rise steeply up or down from the hook shank. For this reason, this knot will not work on hooks with a straight eye. Use a loop knot or an improved clinch knot for those types of hooks.

Salmon fly with down eye tied to the leader with a turtle knot.

Shrimp fly for coastal fly fishing tied on a short shank hook with a straight eye and mounted with a loop knot that will make the fly move enticingly through the waves.

Chapter 11

Practice Makes the Champion

Everyone can pick up and learn something from watching an experienced angler. Orkla, Norway.

Start on the lawn!

A lot of truth lies in the saying that practice makes perfect. Every person who has tried to learn how to play the piano, the tuba, golf, or pool knows this. Or you might have tried to make a pair of downhill skis cooperate or tried to build up the physical stamina to go through a marathon. The message is the same—practice makes perfect.

The same thing goes for fly casting. The good and stable casting technique that we all want doesn't come of its own accord. But the time you spend practicing is time well spent, and you will soon feel your own progress.

Unless you are an experienced fly caster, you should start with overhand casting on a single-handed fly rod (see the exercises in chapter 4). The overhand cast is the foundation for all casts, which is why it is called the basic cast. Practice this cast with a line length of about two rod lengths plus the leader outside the tip guide.

I strongly recommend that you practice your basic skills on a lawn. You might think that the best starting point is to put a fly at the end of the leader and combine your casting practice with the chance of catching a fish in your favorite water, but this is not the case.

Your focus—which is supposed to be on your casting skills—will vanish as soon as you have fish in the water in front of you. Suddenly you also need to take things such as water, bank-side vegetation, and wind into consideration, not to mention a fly that might get stuck in all sorts of possible and impossible places. This kind of practice is absolutely no help. You need to concentrate 100 percent on the whereabouts of line, leader, hands, arms, and rod.

I practice on grass occasionally. A long stretch of green is the optimal place to practice those basic movements, and when you know them even in your sleep, you have the freedom to be flexible in your casting and during practical fishing. When the casting is running smoothly and the fly ends up in the exact right place every time, it gets so much easier to read the water and figure out how the fly moves through it.

Fishing is off-limits!

The English angling writer and Spey casting instructor Hugh Falkus (1917–1996) held a number of casting courses on the famous River Spey. He felt compelled to give the participants strict orders so they did not fall for the temptation to practice casting and fish for salmon at the same time. Falkus simply dictated: "Fishing after breakfast is *verboten* (forbidden)." He even went as far as to ban fly dummies during practice because salmon attacked them several times. And I have to agree with him. When you attempt to practice and fish at the same time, the result is, far too often, that you get no practice at all—and even fewer fish in the bag.

Casting practice and fishing should be kept separate. You have plenty of room in front and behind you for the overhead cast on the lawn. Avoid days with too much wind, because strong moving air will disturb the movements of the cast. Try to practice in conditions that are as neutral as possible.

When you are on the lawn with the tackle ready and a piece of wool at the end of the leader, the only thing you have to worry about is the cast itself. You can focus on performing and studying the casting movement, and put all your energy into the movement of the rod back and forth between the different stop positions. It is a pleasure to follow a rod and line that work well together, which makes it possible to cast the line easily and elegantly with a minimal effort.

Spey casting takes water

Spey casting, on the other hand, cannot be done on grass alone. You will need the surface tension to grab the leader like countless small hands and flex the rod against the resistance. But there is no reason to practice the cast at a fine stream teeming with aggressive salmon jumping around your ears. The bank of a lake will do just fine. When I teach the Scandinavian Spey cast, class often takes place on a stretch of river where no fishing is done so the participants can turn their whole attention to the dynamics of the cast itself.

Practicing the Spey cast on a lake is, in fact, more difficult that practicing on a stream or river. Lakes have no current to pull the line, making the lift much harder to perform correctly. But if you can Spey cast on still water, you will also be able to Spey cast on a stream. And if you get used to the feeling of the current always stretching out your line for you, you might experience problems when you fish the slow stretches of a stream.

You'll find the optimal conditions for learning the Scandinavian Spey cast by wading out a bit so you are clear of reeds, bushes, branches, and rocks along the bank. But do not stand in water up to your thighs, because this will only make the lift harder to do, just as the D-shape behind you will get too narrow to handle. Stand in water to the middle of your shins to take full control of the cast. Also practice the Spey cast standing on the bank, because water is for fishing and not for wading. When you practice Spey casting, you should start with a line long enough to get a reasonable angle on the backcast—about 30 feet of fly line plus 13 feet of leader.

Cast short

Many fly fishers wish that they could cast longer than they can. This desire is understandable; you can find great personal satisfaction in foot upon foot of running line disappearing across the stream.

The reality is, however, that you don't need a record cast to catch fish. In fact, at least 90 percent of all fish taken on a fly rod are caught within the first 75 feet. This does not mean that you will never come across a situation where a long line is needed. And it is nice to know that you actually can put out a long line the day you need it. But keep in mind that a perfect cast is when the leader stretches like it should—and the ultimate perfect cast is one that stretches *and* catches a fish. If your line ends up in a pile halfway to the horizon, those few extra feet of casting are not worth much.

A long cast will give you a poor connection with your fly, and that fly will be hard to control as it moves across the current. So do not cast any longer than you have to, and keep your loop under control. This goes for the practice on the lawn as well as on the stream. And practice is the way to move ahead when fly casting.

Have fun!

Henrik Mortensen

Silver colored and fresh from the sea, the Atlantic salmon is truly a magnificent fish—and nothing feels better than giving it freedom again. Petit Cascapédia, Canada.

Index